The Business Culture in France

The Business Culture in France

Colin Gordon

With contributions by Paul Kingston

BUTTERWORTH
HEINEMANN

Butterworth-Heinemann
Linacre House, Jordan Hill, Oxford OX2 8DP
A division of Reed Educational & Professional Publishing Ltd

℞ A member of the Reed Elsevier plc group

OXFORD   BOSTON   JOHANNESBURG
MELBOURNE   NEW DELHI   SINGAPORE

First published 1996

British Library Cataloguing in Publication Data
Gordon, Colin
  Business Culture in France
  I. Title
  650.0944

ISBN 0 7506 1832 9

Set by Graphicart Typesetters Ltd, Hong Kong
Printed and bound in Great Britain by Clays Ltd, St Ives plc

Contents

Series preface

The need for the present series of country books on business cultures arose from the success of *Business Cultures in Europe*, which was first published in 1990, reprinted in 1991, and went into a second edition in 1993. Thereafter, it was felt that the topic of business culture in the major countries in the European Community (EC) was deserving of a larger canvas than that afforded by a mere chapter. Hence a short series of country books is initially contemplated, beginning with Germany and continuing with further publications on Spain, France and the United Kingdom.

All the books in the series have a number of features in common, the most outstanding of which is probably the need to arrive at a tenable definition of 'business culture'.

If a country's 'culture' can be defined as 'the state of intellectual development among a people', then 'business culture' might be held to be 'the state of commercial development in a country'. But the concept of business culture surely embraces this and much more: it also takes in the beliefs, attitudes and values that underpin commercial activities and help to shape the behaviours of companies in a given country. These companies, in their turn, develop their own individual 'corporate cultures', which, put simply, manifest 'the way we do things round here'.

Implicit in the definition of a country's business culture provided above is the fact that there is no such thing as a single, homogeneous European business culture. Europe contains as many business cultures as it does countries. Although the similarities between the business cultures in Europe are legion, so are the differences.

What are the determinants of the business cultures of European countries? What are the factors affecting the similarities and differences between countries? It is self-evident that the relationship between business and government, the shape and orientation of the economy, the financial institutions, and the trade unions all exert a profound effect on the business cultures of all European countries. But is, for example, the attitude of business to green issues equally significant for the business cultures everywhere in Europe? Is, say, the practice of élitism sufficiently widespread to count as a determinant of business cultures in all European countries? The answer in both cases is 'no'.

In other words, the business culture in a particular country grows partly out of what could be called the 'current business environment' of that country. Yet business culture is a much broader concept because, alongside the impulses that are derived from the present business environment figure the historical experiences of the business community, such as the periods of hyper-inflation in Germany in 1923 and, in the west of the country, again after the Second World War. In Spain the legacy of Francoism is still a phenomenon the business community is striving to overcome. Of equal significance for the business culture are the future hopes and aspirations not only of business but also of society at large in a given country. How long, for example, should people work in any one week in the 1990s and beyond?

The books in the series focus on the business culture of the country concerned in the late 1970s, throughout the 1980s, and into the mid-1990s. The individual chapters in the books concentrate on those determinants of business culture that are held to be significant for the country under review. Some of the determinants are common to all the countries in the series; others are relevant for only one or two.

The authors of the books in the series have not hesitated to use foreign words and concepts in their works, because such expressions contribute much to the depiction of the nuances in the business culture of any country. They have, however, been at pains to provide a translation of the term in the foreign language on its first appearance in the book.

A conscious attempt has been made to use the common statistical base provided by the Organization for Economic Co-operation and Development (OECD) wherever possible, and especially with regard to major economic indicators such as growth rates and inflation, so that the reader can make meaningful comparisons between countries. Where common statistics are not available, reputable national sources have been used. Sources have been indicated for all figures and tables.

Towards the end of every book in the series a list of publications has been provided in the form of sources and suggestions for further reading. Here only standard works or publications have been included that might stimulate the reader to delve deeper into special aspects of the business culture in the country under review. These lists should not be regarded as exhaustive.

The authors trust that an appreciation of the business cultures in the major EC countries will lead to a better understanding of the structures and strategies of industries, markets and consumer preferences in the countries covered in the series. While it may not constitute the most important element of a practitioner's knowledge, cultural fluency in any one country could make that vital difference between actually gaining a contract or merely coming close.

Collin Randlesome

Preface

One single event has overshadowed all others in recent times in France – the election of a new president. Two main reasons made this election as critical and mould-breaking as that of Mitterand in 1981. First, Mitterand had enjoyed a period of fourteen years in power and France was now ready for a change, having become disillusioned and cynical about politics and politicians. Ceaseless and increasing bouts of corruption, together with rising unemployment and inequalities in the spread of wealth were threatening the very existence of the Socialist party, undermined even further by Mitterand's wrecking Machiavellian plots over his successor.

Secondly, a new president was confronted with a France which, although economically and industrially, it was arguable, sound, was nevertheless in need of urgent solutions to a number of problems which had festered like boils in need of lancing. The poison was and is unemployment which, at 12.3 per cent of the working population, is half as much again as in the UK and Germany. The causes are many and complex but, when the effects of recession and economic policy are stripped out they are essentially structural: more young people and women coming into the labour market when growth is barely able to stabilize unemployment let alone create a surplus of new jobs; hiring and firing practices which make companies wary of taking on new employees; a minimum wage which prices unskilled labour out of a job; trade union attitudes of resistance to the privatization and deregulation which could revitalize the economy; and high social security charges which cause companies to pause for thought before hiring. The general picture is one of a highly regulated labour market in which companies find ample reasons to make do with existing labour.

Not that economic policy over the last years can be exonerated of blame. French growth rates in the 1960s – towards the end of **les Trente Glorieuses**, the thirty glorious years of almost uninterrupted growth between 1945 and 1975 – and even in the 1970s, constantly outshone those of its competitors. In nine out of the last twelve years, they have trailed behind, and many economic experts would point the finger of blame at the strong franc (**le franc fort**) policy which over the majority of those years has anchored the franc firmly to the German mark and to the high interest rates resulting from German reunification. Indeed, although the new president is likely to reaffirm the 'franc policy', there are nevertheless dissenting voices in his own ranks clamouring for the **option britannique**, devaluation and withdrawal from the European Monetary System (EMS). Such a dramatic U-turn is barely conceivable, however, given the deep-seated need France feels to tie Germany into closer European integration through European Monetary Union (EMU).

Here, too, however, the poison erupts again as the new president, Jacques Chirac, promises to tackle unemployment but faces the conundrum of how to do this, whilst slashing the budgetary deficit down from its current 5.7 per cent of GDP to the 3 per cent required to qualify for EMU. Cuts in services or increases in taxation hardly square with increased employment. The postponement of EMU until 1999 is unlikely to buy Chirac the time to accomplish what appears to be a precarious balancing act.

On the privatization front, progress has been slowed by the poor performance of the Paris Bourse which is particularly open to the ebb and flow of foreign investment funds, with over one-third of traded securities being in the hands of overseas investors, in particular American pension funds. Although few contest the economic and industrial need for privatization in France, trade union resistance to changes in employee status and a shift in the balance of power – the majority of the union power base in terms of membership is in the state-owned sector – is having a major influence on the speed and precise nature of individual privatizations. In the case of Renault, the state remains the majority shareholder, a situation foreseen by Volvo and undoubtedly a contributory factor to the failure of the proposed Volvo–Renault merger. The model is likely to be repeated in the privatization of other candidates and points to the apparent paradox of the strength of the trade union movement in spite of its low membership and fragmentation.

As will be seen, part of this strength resides in the role the main unions play in the co-management of the social security system, the cost of which is another underlying cause of unemployment and requires all the new president's skills to unbundle (in the absence of big tax increases or welfare reforms, France's public debt could rise to 88 per cent of GDP by the year 2030, according to an OECD report). By insisting on over-generous increases and changes in the system, the unions have been seen to gain the upper hand over employers and the task of Jean Gandois, another new president, this time of the employers' confederation, the CNPF, is to redress the balance. One of his immediate moves was to meet with the unions in an attempt to lay out a new employers' stall and achieve the delicate task of working, albeit more muscularly than his predecessor, with unions historically averse to any significant form of cooperation, particularly over **avantages acquis**, rights to social and work-related benefits which are so fiercely defended in France.

Reform of the social security system and its costs must be high on the agenda of Chirac's measures to combat unemployment. Steps had already been taken under the previous prime minister, Balladur, to lengthen the number of years' service qualifying for the state-run pension schemes and the very first pension funds are beginning to emerge. More stringent controls of expenditure on prescribed medicines have been introduced and the charge levied on companies to pay for family allowances is gradually being removed. These are marginal, however, to the central issue of taxation reform which must be undertaken to be fairer and more efficient. Income tax is only paid by 50 per cent of families and calculated in a painfully complicated way. There is no PAYE (pay-as-you-earn) scheme and tax evasion is probably widespread. Taxation of companies at local level – the **taxe professionnelle** – also needs overhaul in that it, too, is a job tax, being calculated, amongst other factors, on the basis of numbers employed.

Unemployment has hit all categories of the French workforce, including the managerial grade of **cadre**, hitherto considered to be largely protected and immune to job-cutting measures. The consequent loss of morale amongst managers has hence been considerable in a country where they have often been likened to a privileged caste, a meritocratic aristocracy which spearheaded France's economic and industrial revival after the Second World War. Their education and training compound this élitist view and, although now available to a greater number through the creation of more engineering schools (engineer and manager being so often synonymous in France), the general view is that the bias towards the highly competitive business and engineering schools will continue to the detriment of the non-selective universities.

The young élite are now beginning to recover and find employment but at the other end of the scale those with low or no qualifications find the bar is set too high in the contest for a job. France has, therefore, the highest youth unemployment figure (25 per cent) of the G7 group of countries. Employment schemes are accordingly being especially geared to the unqualified, both young and middle-aged, with France again having one of the highest number of long-term unemployed (1 million plus).

France requires change, then, but is nevertheless fundamentally strong from a number of points of view. Its trade balance has shown a strong surplus since 1993, albeit largely due to reduced consumer demand but underlining the fact that, in spite of high social security costs, French industry remains competitive. Growth is forecast to quicken to 3.5 per cent in 1995 and 3 per cent in 1996. The franc remains at the bottom end of the permitted band of the EMS but more due to political uncertainties than to weak economic fundamentals. France is the fourth largest economy in the world and also the fourth biggest exporter.

There is much that is positive, therefore, but in spite of this, the French themselves feel and express a continuing malaise. Part of this, as they themselves admit, is due to their **râleur** tradition (**râler** = to moan or gripe) and to a feeling that since the Trente Glorieuses (akin to Macmillan's 'you've never had it so good' era) there has been a period of continuing economic and social 'crisis' (**la crise**). Disaffection with politicians, a view shared by many that a single European market is at the expense of French jobs, concern over immigrants, particularly North Africans (immigration = crime) and mounting anxiety over the spread of Islam, as France keeps a close watch on events in Algeria, have all been factors in the recent renaissance of the National Front in local government elections. So often dismissed as extremist and abusive misfits whose main appeal was to the disaffected, a recent development has been the emergence of candidates with highly professional and managerial backgrounds who have been elected mayors of a few major cities, notably Toulon. They can, therefore, no longer be dismissed as mere rabble-rousers but must be taken as serious contenders to win the hearts and minds of many French who are expressing frustration over crime, immigration and unemployment. Most of the main political parties and media view this trend with dismay and distaste but some are viewing it as a warning that, unless tangible inroads are made into unemployment, French society could undergo serious splits.

This, too, is a challenge facing the new president, the leader of an over-whelmingly right-wing government with the socialist party still founder-ing in spite of the strong showing of Lionel Jospin in the presidential elections. The voice of the discontented must be heard if extremist, xenophobic factions are to be contained. As far as French business is con-cerned, against the background of some reasonably sound indicators, if there is a threat, it is likely to be on the social front, with the ever-present risk of a social explosion, unless unemployment is seriously tackled.

Reproduced from Gladkow, J. and Sanders, C. (1991), *Franc Exchange* by permission of Addison-Wesley, Longman Ltd

1   Business and government

Introduction

More than in any other OECD country, the state has played a crucial and all-pervasive role in France in determining the major directions in which business activities have moved. **Interventionniste, dirigiste, colbertiste** (after Louis XIV's minister Colbert, who directly or indirectly controlled much of the country's economy) are words which are frequently used to sum up a habit which dies hard, even in a period of right-wing government which professes to be a believer in the market economy and in privatization. Indeed, France's present economic and industrial situation, after a prolonged recession, is set against a backcloth of harsh European and world market realities which are seriously laying bare the corporatism and introspection encouraged by a state only too ready to mollycoddle and put off tough decisions.

Central government

Three features in particular stand out when examining the influence central government has exercised on business since the Second World War. First, the importance, now much diminished, attached to a system of so-called indicative five-year economic plans, especially during the Trente Glorieuses (1945–1975), the thirty 'glorious' years of growth. Secondly, largely in response to the former West German economic miracle, the American challenge of the 1960s and for reasons of national independence, in terms of technology, natural resources and of defence, the French authorities devised a system of industrial policies specifically designed both to convert inefficient industries and develop those it considered of strategic importance, particularly in high-tech sectors. These took the form of mergers and takeovers engineered by a policy of tax incentives, nationalizations (even by right-wing governments), medium- and long-term credits channelled through a state-directed financial sector and guarantees of government supply contracts. This was the policy of 'national champions' and such present-day companies as Alcatel-Alstholm, Péchiney, Saint-Gobain, Rhône-Poulenc, and SNIAS (Aérospatiale) were all moulded during the heyday of this period in the 1970s and early 1980s. Thirdly, the fact that from 1958 until 1981 France enjoyed an uninterrupted period of one-party rule, the rise of the Socialist party as a possible alternative government being of quite recent date – the early 1970s.

The initial plans were limited to building up industry after the devastation of war but in the boom years of the 1960s they became so sophisticated and comprehensive – they quantified not only all macro-economic variables but industrial inputs and outputs – that they generated much interest abroad and France was considered to have discovered the secret of managing effectively the complexities of a national economy. Indeed, a Hudson Institute report of the early 1970s proclaimed France as the 'potential Japan' of Europe. Internal crises – the return of one million **pieds noirs**, the white settlers of Algeria, in 1962, for example – and international constraints such as that imposed by the first oil shock, eventually blew some of the later plans off course. Planning lost much of its quantifying importance except as a framework for pushing through, unfettered by annual budgetary constraints, huge technological ventures such as equipping France with a new digitalized telephone system – **grands projets** of breadth and vision initiated and backed by the state which have typified France's approach to technology. The Channel Tunnel is the latest of such projects and the enthusiasm with which it has been greeted in France as a technlogical feat contrasts sharply with British scepticism over safety and complaints about cost.

The middle and late 1970s were typified by erratic stop–go policies implemented in reaction to the new conditions of reduced growth – the beginning of *la crise*, a continual state of uncertainty and a word which punctuates economic analysis even today as if until 1974, France, to borrow Harold Macmillan's words, 'had never had it so good'. Under ex-president Giscard d'Estaing and his prime minister, Jacques Chirac, growth slumped to –2 per cent in 1975 (the first minus figure since the war), investment fell sharply and both bankruptcies and unemployment increased dramatically. Under Raymond Barre, Chirac's successor, there was an attempt both to combat the immediate crisis with an austerity programme of higher taxation and a temporary freeze on wages and prices and to initiate a longer-term restructuring of the economy to bring it more into line with the country which increasingly became France's benchmark, former West Germany. Such a policy involved increasing reluctance to support lame duck industries and the result was a dramatically high level of unemployment ($1\frac{1}{2}$ million in 1981). Nor did the austerity programme reduce inflation (13 per cent in 1980). The franc held steady, however, due partially to a growth rate slightly above the Western average (GDP grew by

$1^1/_2$ per cent in 1980). A healthy surplus in the trade balance was wiped out by the second oil crisis of 1979, a year which also marked the beginning of France's membership of the new European Monetary System, ultimately to become the bedrock of its economic policy and its commitment to anchorage to the German mark.

High levels of inflation and unemployment and a growing trade deficit – this, then, was the situation inherited by the incoming Socialist government in a fraught alliance with the Communists, with François Mitterand as president. There is some argument about the opportuneness of the **programme commun** (a common political platform with the communists) including a policy of reflation which he then decided to pursue. Most observers consider that reflation against the current of a severe world recession was akin to hara-kiri. Others, particularly many French themselves, deem it to have been purely unlucky in its timing. Certainly, its objectives were clear and heralded by euphoric supporters as a new dawn for economic and social policy in France, increased growth, a reduction in unemployment and wage differentials, and maintenance of purchasing power. To achieve these objectives, there was an increase in the **SMIC** (minimum wage) and social benefits, a reduction in the legal working week to 39 hours, retirement for all at 60, and a fifth paid week of annual leave – a heady cocktail which rapidly led to increased labour and therefore production costs. Yet more inflation was inevitable and the resulting loss of competitiveness of French industry combined with the increase in demand fuelled a chronic trade balance deficit and three devaluations of the franc. On a number of occasions, France was near to the point of withdrawing from the EMS. For the business world, the effects were catastrophic. Profits and investment levels had already been steadily declining throughout the 1970s and the recourse to crippling bank borrowing to cover ever-increasing costs led to a lack of profitability from which companies emerged in the mid-to-late 1980s.

One other aspect of the joint Socialist–Communist *programme commun* must be mentioned, the extension of the already considerable state-owned industrial and financial sectors. Ideology no doubt played its part but there was also some sincerity in the conviction that private industry had failed to invest in the 1970s and that the state would have to take control, if France was to maintain a powerful industrial presence in the world, with the necessary financial support to sustain it.

Nationalization was no stranger to France. Whereas the issue aroused passionate opposition in the British parliament in the immediate post-war years, a similar programme in France during the same period provoked little ideological debate, a dirigiste industrial policy (whether through planning or nationalization) becoming an acceptable, even desirable, norm to back up private industry. Even under the continuing domination of parties of the right in government, and particularly during the 'national champion' years of the 1970s, rationalization via takeovers by existing state companies continued unabated. Despite their shortcomings the existence of state companies was never challenged, particularly since investment was considerably greater in the state than in the private sector (especially in energy and telecommunications) and many firms depended on it as subcontractors. Indeed, the notion itself of state-owned is difficult to define, enmeshed as it is in the mechanisms available to execute the Plans, subsidies, advantageous state contracts and the ability of state-owned companies to attract private investors (up to 49 per cent of their capital, using **certificats d'investissement**, non-voting stock). Germany had its banks playing a big role as sources of corporate finance, the UK and America had stock markets but France found itself in between, with the state providing funding, even markets, in a so-called 'mixed economy' of interdependent private and public ownership.

But in 1982–3, the process of state ownership reached its zenith with eventually, in 1984, the public sector representing:

- 16 per cent of the working population (excluding agriculture and government departments)
- 28 per cent of turnover
- 36 per cent of investment
- 23 per cent of exports
- 91 per cent of bank deposits.

The whole vast experiment of the early Socialist years failed catastrophically, however, and in 1983, the Socialists were forced to execute a spectacular U-turn by introducing a series of austerity measures (the Delors Plan), including a reduction in public expenditure and the tightening of exchange controls. A particular body blow was dealt to households with a compulsory loan of 10 per cent of their previous tax payments and a special tax of 10 per cent of taxable income to finance the social security system. Prices and incomes had already been frozen in 1982, an event which was to mark the beginning of a process of negotiation of annual salaries between employers and unions designed to halt the indexation of salaries whereby there were quarterly increases which anticipated future price rises. A reduction of inflation and the restoration of company profits were the main priorities during the 1983–6 period and these were achieved both through government action (containment of tax rises and budget deficit below 3 per cent of GDP) and through the windfall of a drop in oil prices.

Many jobs created in the state sector were precisely those to go first, and perhaps the true significance of the U-turn was the new-found belief by the Socialists that only companies, not the state, could create wealth and therefore jobs. This was indeed a major break with the past. Austerity taught that economic policy could no longer guarantee social progress, and the ideals of the consumer society and the promises of politicians took a back seat to harsh economic realities, to be controlled and rectified by the mandarins of government departments. Companies had been forced to bear the brunt of *la crise* through giving in to inflationary salary demands (the share of added value going to salaries had increased rapidly in the 1970s and early 1980s). Indeed, two major tenets of economic policy under the Fifth Republic were social regulation through inflation and full employment. Productivity was now the major determinant of salary increases whereas in the past the adjustment of salaries to the cost of living was anticipated, in the name of social harmony. The French had thus grown used to inflation as an automatic guarantor of the increase in their wealth and it is in this light that the importance of the de-indexation of salaries should be seen. As for unemployment, this was now inevitable with austerity. But for a left-wing party this was an astonishing discovery and about-face, and its acceptance of this new reality and the necessity to face up to *la crise* were key factors in kindling a reconciliation between the French and the world of business. They realized that profit mattered and was desirable. To be competitive sufficient profit margins and hence lower labour costs were needed, and inflationary wage demands could only act as a brake. The automatic link between technical progress, profit and salaries was broken.

By the time of the general election in 1986, then, the economy was being nursed back to health, with the slower rate of increase in labour costs and the fall in imported raw material prices gradually contributing to lower inflation. Reduced demand plus an effective policy to reduce energy imports through the substitution of nuclear energy (80 per cent of electricity in France is now generated by nuclear means) transformed the trade deficit in both goods and services into a surplus by 1986.

The new right-wing government under Jacques Chirac (with a Socialist president still in power, however) was an ardent advocate of less state spending, deregulation and liberalization. Privatization of not only the newly nationalized companies but also of those which had been in the state sector since immediately before or after the war, became a burning issue, with CGE (later to change its name to Alcatel-Alstholm) and Saint Gobain (glass) in the industrial sector, Société Générale and Paribas in banking, Agence Havas (advertising) and the television channel TF1 reverting to private hands before the October crash of 1987.

Liberalization in particular meant a dismantling of supply-side rigidities, especially the necessity for companies to seek the authorization of the local Inspector of Labour before shedding labour, reduction in taxation and total freedom in prices except for pharmaceutical and oil products. The reduction of the government deficit, business efficiency and market forces became the driving forces and many in France, with its long tradition of dirigisme, became concerned whether those were right policies for France. The stock market crash of 1987 only compounded these fears and reinforced the widespread belief in France that the stock exchange (**la Bourse**) was for speculators, like a gambling casino. Indeed, De Gaulle had once said that 'economic policy could not be dictated by the Bourse'.

The highest marginal rate of personal income tax fell from 72.4 per cent in 1986 to 56.8 per cent in 1988, the rate of corporation tax was reduced from 50 per cent to 42 per cent (now 34 per cent) and the payroll tax (**taxe professionnelle**) was progressively cut. Offset against this, however, social insurance contributions were increased in 1987 and these, combined with other forms of taxation, both direct and indirect, contribute to France having the heaviest burden of taxes among the major OECD countries (43.8 per cent of GDP in 1990, 36.5 per cent in the UK). This is still of some considerable concern as the social security system creaks under the weight of an ever-more-costly pay-as-you-go scheme which has the effect of restricting employment (see Chapter 5).

The resolve to continue a public sector pay policy which had a knock-on effect in the private sector increasingly provided business with greater profits and hence with the investment levels of the early 1970s. Unemployment still stubbornly refused to fall, however, as growth in 1986 remained sluggish when France failed to take as much advantage of the upturn in the world economy as other OECD countries. Fear of another dramatic turn of events as witnessed in 1983, together with a strong franc policy through the chastening discipline of membership of the EMS and being hence locked into former West Germany's own meagre growth performance, forestalled any idea of expansion through reflation.

In 1988, President Mitterand was elected for a second term and a general election was called. Chirac's popularity had faded, perhaps due to the 1987 stock market crash which disillusioned many who had believed shares only went up in value but had found that the opposite was also true. There was no panic selling but the government no doubt suffered the fall-out from the episode. In the election, a landslide victory was predicted for the Socialists but they surprisingly failed to win an overall majority and were forced to seek the support of members of the centrist parties. The party's popularity slumped severely, however, particularly under the Prime Ministership of Edith Cresson, who managed to antagonize most sections of public opinion with both strident and ill-advised remarks and a penchant for a heavy-handed dose of interventionist industrial policy.

President Mitterand fared little better, being wrong-footed by the coup attempt in Moscow (which he supported), the unification of Germany (which he opposed) and the Gulf War (when he wavered). He was seen as increasingly out of touch and losing his grip on both domestic and world events, and there were demands for a reduction in the presidential term from seven to five years. With the steadying hand of the new prime minister, Pierre Bérégooy, the architect of the strong franc and competitive disinflation policy, Mitterand bounced back to some degree, however, but not enough to save the Socialist party from defeat in the national elections in 1993. The party was rocked by accusations of corruption, particularly at local level where, to swell party fund coffers, various favours (such as planning permission) had been accorded to companies in return for handsome donations. In addition, there was a widespread lack of faith in a socialist party which, during its reign, had seen unemployment rates soar and the gap between the rich and the poor grow larger. Finally, France had slumped into only its second bout of recession since the Second World War (GDP shrank by –1.2 per cent in 1993) as membership of the EMS tied the country to punitive interest rates to stay in tandem with German rates pushed higher by the miscalculated cost of reunification. Unemployment climbed to 12.0 per cent with the very real threat of worse to come in 1994. Inflation stood firm, however, and there were signs that a trade deficit would be turned into a surplus as household consumption slumped.

The right-wing parties, the UDF (**Union pour la Démocratie Française**) and the RPR (**Rassemblement pour la République**) under the leadership respectively of Valéry Giscard d'Estaing and Jacques Chirac, swept to power in the March elections of 1993 with a huge majority. The prime minister, Edouard Balladur, claimed to have inherited the worst economic mess since the war. In addition to the gloomy figures on growth and unemployment, the budget deficit was growing to a record 410 bn Ffr. After two economic packages matters seemed to be even worse but through it all and despite both calls from sections of his own government for the **option britannique** – slashing of interest rates, exit from the EMS and devaluation of the franc – and a heavy run on the franc in August of 1993, leading to a widening of the EMS bands to 15 per cent, Balladur stood firm and seemed to be vindicated by a very gradual easing of interest rates in Germany and hence in France at the latter end of 1993 and the beginning of 1994. Investment is still at a low level, however, in spite of signs of an end to the recession. The one bright spot is provided by trade figures which show a ballooning surplus, due to increased exports, proving that in spite of complaints over the level of labour costs due to high social charges, certain sectors of French industry have regained their competitiveness (Figures 1.1, 1.2).

For the first four months of 1994, foreign trade showed a surplus of 23.5 bn Ffr, after a record surplus in 1993 of 89.6 bn Ffr, completing a run of three years (including 1994) of surpluses after thirty years during which deficits have been the rule. Two-thirds of trade is with the European Union with major strengths being in agriculture (cereals), capital

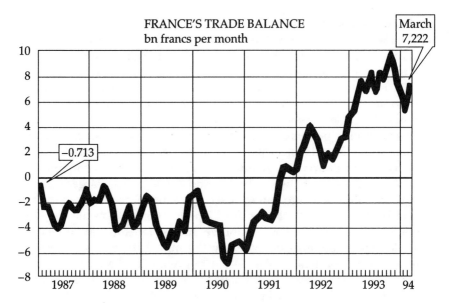

Figure 1.1   *France's trade balance. Source: OECD*

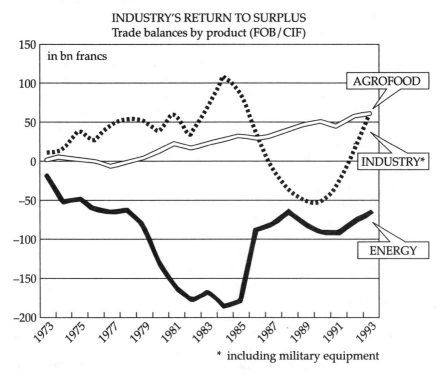

Figure 1.2   *Industry's return to surplus. Source: Customs*

goods, military equipment and vehicles, and weaknesses in energy, raw materials and consumer goods (particularly electronic).

Privatizations

In industrial policy terms, Mitterand had declared in 1988 that there would be no more nationalizations nor privatizations and that a mixed economy would prevail, giving the best of both worlds. Nevertheless, companies in the state sector could now seek up to 49 per cent private capital, an increase from the previous level of 25 per cent. In addition, in spite of Mitterand's *'ni-ni'* policy, 14 per cent of the chemical company Rhône-Poulenc's capital was floated in a partial privatization in 1992.

Part of the right-wing government's election manifesto focused on a further and massive bout of privatizations, however, to pick up from the uncompleted previous round of the 1986–8 government. No one in France now argues over the necessity to privatize. Even the Socialists, as Balladur bitingly puts it, having nationalized for employment, now want to privatize to fight against unemployment. For, in brutal terms, the state needs the money, particularly for unemployment schemes. In addition, the EC Commission is becoming increasingly impatient with France's frequent injections of capital into some of its ailing companies, such as Bull, the computer manufacturer, and Air France. The discussion is more over the timetable, which companies should be sold first, shareholding structures and what is to happen to the monopolies in the public service sector, e.g. EDF–GDF (Electricité de France – Gaz de France), France Télécom and the French railways, SNCF. The target set for privatization receipts in 1993 was 40 bn Ffr and 30–50 bn Ffr in subsequent years, with the proceeds to go towards public housing, rebuilding the balance sheets of the privatized companies and repayment of public debt.

The scene is set for the centre of gravity of French capitalism to change. The whole of French industry will be affected by privatization, given the size of state-owned companies' holdings in private companies (Figure 1.3).

Twenty-one companies are on the government's published list (Table 1.1), representing 1 million employees, 1,200 bn Ffr turnover and several thousand subsidiary companies. The market economy and competition are now more important than companies belonging to state control. The effect of this radical transformation has been likened by François Morin, Professor at the University of Toulouse-1, to a veritable earthquake with two shock waves, the first affecting the relationships between state companies themselves and the second, relationships between state and private companies whose growth had depended on injections of public capital.

In the case of state companies such as Thomson and Bull, if they are privatized, the state still retains a big stake via state-owned Crédit

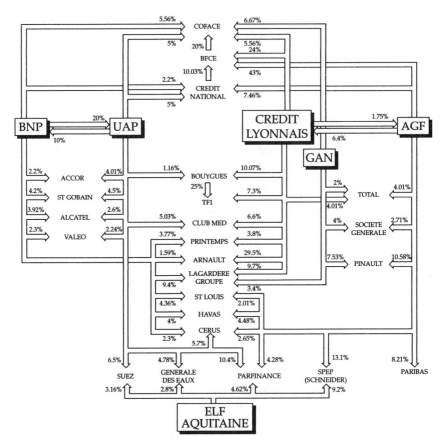

Figure 1.3 *Privatizable companies and the private sector. Source: Le Monde, 28.7.93*

Lyonnais and Elf (Figure 1.4), underlying the whole paradoxical nature of privatizations whereby companies may be privatized but not their shareholders. In the case of the privatization of Péchiney and Rhône-Poulenc, their main shareholders are also privatizable and conflicts of power and interest may arise if they form part of different alliances when privatized. The same is true of Aérospatiale in which Crédit Lyonnais has a 20 per cent stake. The company which eventually controls Crédit Lyonnais will have a clear say in the affairs of Aérospatiale. But it goes further. Crédit Lyonnais is 24.19 per cent owned by Thomson, 25 per cent of which is owned by France Telecom. There is hence likely to be a whole domino effect on the future of Aérospatiale unless the state demands the selling off of their various stakes before companies are privatized.

Much depends on the **noyaux durs** (hard core) policy. Back in 1986, in the first wave of privatization there were cries of foul when a *noyau dur* of stable shareholders friendly to the government was found to invest

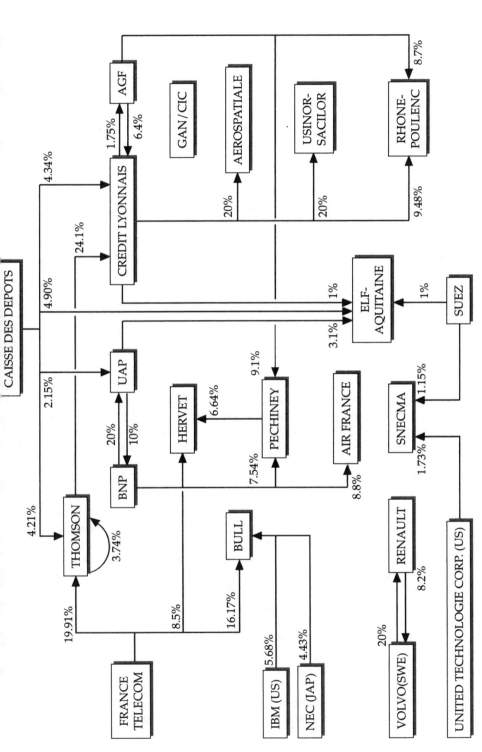

Figure 1.4 *State company cross-shareholdings. Source: Le Monde, 3.9.93*

in the newly privatized companies. This time round, a special privatization commission consisting of seven members will invite bids and from these recommend new 'noyaux durs', constituting up to 25–30 per cent of capital. The government then has the right to accept or reject the recommendation. Interest will focus on whether the government decides to fragment these stable shareholders or group them around a major 'reference' shareholder (**actionnaire de référence**) as could well be the case with Aérospatiale.

Initial plans not to place a ceiling on foreign investors were dismissed in favour of a 20 per cent limit on non-EC investors. No such limit exists for EC investors, however, as this would contravene Community Single Market legislation. A golden share (**action spécifique**) was also introduced, which would allow agreements to be given to groups exceeding shareholding thresholds. It will also entitle the state to nominate one or two board members and to veto the selling of shares considered to be against the national interest. Any holding exceeding 5 per cent in the health, security and defence sectors will require the agreement of the Minister of the Economy. No time limit has been placed on the golden share.

In most cases, a populist floating is envisaged but not with the same level of hype as in 1986 which did so much to raise expectations of quick profits. In spite of the chastening experience of Black Wednesday when many deserted the Bourse, France nevertheless still numbers 5.8 million individual shareholders (**les petits porteurs**) – a far cry, however, from the period around the First World War when the Bourse attracted so many more small punters, and investing in shares was akin to betting on horses or playing roulette.

In the telecommunications, electricity and gas sectors, European directives provide for far-reaching deregulation in 1998 and the French companies most affected, France Télécom, Electricité de France (EDF) and Gaz de France, being still state-owned, find themselves ill-prepared for the shift from the calm anchorage of dependable domestic markets to the open seas of deregulation and the resulting tougher competition.

In the case of France Télécom, which hitherto has had no serious competitors in its home market, considerable upset has already been caused amongst the workforce through the company's transformation from an **établissement public autonome** into a limited company, a **Société Anonyme**, governed by private law but with the majority of its shares owned by the state (51 per cent). A move was made once before to change its status but ran into fierce opposition from the principal unions, FO, CFDT, CGT and CFTC. This time, the company was quick to consult the unions first with the reassurance that privatization was not the aim, as France Télécom did not figure on the list of twenty-one companies to be privatized (see Table 1.1). The company will remain in state hands

Table 1.1 *The twenty-one privatizable companies*

Company	Turnover (bn Ffr)	Result (m Ffr)	No. employed	% of state ownership	Date of nationalization	Chairman
Aérospatiale	52.30	−2,380	45,000	74	August 1936	Louis Gallois
Air France	57.20	−3,266	64,000	99	June 1945	Bernard Attali
Banque Hervet	1.10	−186	1,380	55	February 1982	Patrick Careil
BNP	39.90	+2,200	58,000	73	December 1945	Michel Pébereau
Caisse cent. de réassurance.	3.07	+245	160	100	April 1946	Alexis Ruset
Bull	30.10	−4,700	35,200	72	February 1982	Bernard Pache
Compagnie gén. maritime	7.40	−733	2,500	100	July 1933	Eric Giully
Crédit lyonnais	48.90	−1,800	70,000	52	December 1945	Jean-Yves Haberer
Pechiney	65.30	+203	61,000	55	February 1982	Jean Gandois
Renault	179.40	+5,680	146,600	80	January 1945	Louis Schweitzer
Rhône-Poulenc	81.70	+2,200	83,300	43	February 1982	Jean-René Fourtou
AGF	59.40	+1,500	22,000	65	April 1946	Michel Albert
GAN	44	+402	49,000	79	April 1946	François Heilbronner
UAP	126	+1,100	40,000	53	April 1946	Jean Peyrelevade
Seita	13.40	+367	5,500	100	January 1959	Bertrand de Gallé
Société mars. de crédit	3.95	−454	2,368	100	February 1982	Jean Matouk
SNECMA	22.80	−794	25,300	97	May 1945	Géréard Renon
Elf-Aquitaine	200.60	+6,200	87,000	51	November 1941	Loïk Le Floch-Prigent
Thomson	71.30	−544	100,000	82	February 1982	Alain Gomez
Usinor-Sacilor	86.70	−2,400	90,800	80	November 1981	Francis Mer
Caisse nat. de prévoyance	42	+1,120	2,000	42	July 1868	Pierre Darnis

and the workforce will continue to enjoy the same guarantees as before, i.e. as public sector employees, and the myriad of benefits they enjoy, particularly job security. The change has been made necessary, however, primarily to enable France Telecom to seek the alliances which are now imperative for all telecommunications operators as large corporate customers increasingly need global services, particularly in data transmission. British Telecom (BT) has already formed such an alliance with AT&T's principal rival, the American company MCI. France Télécom was already shaping up for an alliance with MCI but the deal was stolen literally from under its nose by BT, a move seen by France Télécom as a resounding defeat caused by its state-owned status and because the domestic market in France is still closed to foreign competitors. It considers that it is vital to have capital which can be opened up to other private operators. Crucial, too, is freedom to use profits for its own purposes and not to be used as the perpetual cash-cow of the state, creamed for money for investment in so-called 'strategic' areas such as the electronics industry, for providing capital for the two state insurance companies, AGF and UAP, and even for the government's own budget.

France Télécom already has one alliance, however, with Deutsche Bundespost Telekom (DBT) in the form of two jointly owned subsidiaries, EUCOM for data transmission and EUNETCOM, networks. As DBT opens up its capital in 1996, crossed shareholdings are likely between the French and German companies, thus making them powerful competitors of the Americans. The aim is to develop a pan-European telecommunications network to help the growth and competition of companies in Europe, thus providing another example, this time in the industrial sector, of the close Franco-German cooperation in shaping the future of Europe. BT sees any agreement as an attempt to exclude it from competition on the continent and provides a clear example of the Anglo-Saxon view of liberalized deregulated markets leading to greater competition clashing with the French view that deregulation is to be viewed with caution, that markets are imperfect and need some form of control and supervision. As unemployment grows in France, such a view enjoys widespread credence and provides a reminder of the increasing disillusionment felt with the Single Market and the inevitable job losses it entails through restructurings made necessary by greater competition and deregulation.

EDF and GDF find themselves in a similar situation where likely union reaction, particularly after the Air France débacle, informs any debate over changes in their status and particularly any suggestion of privatization. There is deep-felt union hostility to European proposals to end the monopolies laid down in the 1946 Act which provided for the notion of public service. The Mandil report, however, recommends an end to EDF's production monopoly and the abolition of EDF and GDF's exclusive rights to the export and import of electricity and gas, to bring France into line with community law and recognize the growing internationalization of the two operators. Transportation and distribution are not to be deregulated, however. A number of private French companies have for long been demanding to be allowed to produce electricity in excess of the 8 megawatt mini power stations at present authorized by law. The main protagonists, Lyonnaise des Eaux-Dumez and Générale des Eaux, point to the increasing encroachment being made by EDF into such areas as waste disposal and urban heating, not only in France but also overseas. Regulation is now being considered by a government embarrassed by its reluctance to deregulate the electricity and gas industries but quite prepared to allow state-backed EDF, particularly, to tread on the toes of private companies in areas open to keen competition. The situation has been brought to a head by EDF's awareness that the writing is on the wall for its monopoly and that one way of keeping its customer base in the future was to propose a whole range of services, a strategy which brought it face to face with the two water conglomerates dominating the sector of services to local communities. Officially, the subsidiaries of EDF responsible for such services are under an obligation not to merge with the parent company and to have totally separate accounts but the suspicion must linger of the possibility of cross-subsidies.

Yet perhaps the episode which has best crystallized the pain France is to undergo as it attempts to find ways of facing up to the reality of competition and thereby rid itself of the negative aspects of Colbert's legacy is the attempt by Air France to take the necessary steps to counteract the debilitating effects of recession. The airline was overmanned and incurring high costs, having lost a record 32 bn Ffr in 1992 and a similar amount in 1993. It is saddled with 21 bn Ffr of debts but, more important, it has gradually lost market share over the last 10 years, except on small African routes, with the biggest fall occurring on the North Atlantic routes. Drastic measures were required, including a cut in the workforce of 2,500 in 1994, after losses of 5,000 over the last few years. The latest plan in the autumn of 1993 met with strident hostility from the workforce and, ultimately, after a period of violent conflict, the management was forced to withdraw it, after the government intervened and failed to back the toughness of the head of Air France, Bernard Attali.

The incident is interesting from a number of points of view. First, it gave the lie to the oft-heard assertion that the government took a hands-off approach to nationalized companies in France, within the overall framework of five-year planning contracts. Attali had no option other than to resign when the minister of transport assumed complete charge of negotiations with the workforce, as the government took fright that the conflagration could spread to other nationalized companies. Secondly, it underlined the social upheaval to come as the government attempts to change the status of companies and therefore, by extension, the status of the workforce, particularly in so far as it affects the guarantee of a job for life. Thirdly, it was highly symbolic in a France bogged down economically and socially, where the risk increases daily of yet more sections of the population being excluded from the world of work and society in general. If the government is to slim down its overmanned public sector, both in readiness for privatization and to stem increasing lack of competitiveness, its tactics will have to be revised. The scale of the problem is immense and not unlike the situation created over the dockers and particularly the miners in the UK in the early 1980s.

The crucial difference between the two situations is the volatility of the French public, the readiness to resort to violent protest and demonstration, a right granted by the Constitution. It would be hard to exaggerate the 'revolutionary' blood coursing in French veins and indeed much of France's social legislation and change has often been the result of an eruption of this constantly active volcano of latent discontent and passion. To call the prime minister's action 'soft' in backing down is to misunderstand completely the nature of the French psyche. Competition, deregulation and greater productivity are needed but the crucial question is at what speed. Against a backcloth of a rapidly deteriorating social scene, concessions have to be made on both sides in a macho confrontation where a win–win solution is vital, where the risk of an all-out social explosion is all too apparent. On the other hand, the corporatist behaviour of certain sections of the workforce needs a firm hand, with the government showing its sure intention of pushing through change. In particular, the privileged status of the state-sector workforce needs pruning but this strikes at the very heart of the problem where job losses only concern a few but cuts in privileges affect all. Indeed, the strikers at Air France said little on the subject of the 4,000 job losses planned but concentrated their attention on the loss of their own privileges! An omnipresent state, therefore, finds itself up a blind alley, where to tackle workers' privileges to avoid redundancies might lead to conflict but where resorting to new waves of job cuts only leads to feeding yet more unemployment, exclusion and desperation.

The unions are not alone in expressing their concerns over Europe. Jacques Fournier, the out-going chairman of the French railways company, SNCF, deplores the wave of liberalism emanating from Brussels in its attempt to break down regulated and monopolistic sectors. In May 1994, the French government refused to bow to Brussels' insistence that it allow foreign airlines to use Orly airport in Paris, hitherto only served by French airlines. As the impact of the Single Market truly begins to make itself felt, unions, the government and captains of industry are only now realizing that the dirigiste state can no longer hold sway even over the public sector, so long at the heart of French Colbertism. Fears of the imposition of the model of Anglo-American capitalism, embedded in notions of free markets and unfettered competition, are bound to temper the confidence France had in a united Europe, as it sees its own model, a kind of European Colbertism, failing to have any appeal, even to its erstwhile partner in Europe, Germany.

Another sign that, in spite of privatization, the state still intends, in the words of André Fontaine, the ex-editor of *Le Monde*, 'to keep a firm hand on the tiller guiding the course of national development', is the manner in which new chairmen were appointed to head up state companies immediately prior to privatization. Three of Balladur's closest advisers, Pébéreau, Jaffré and Friedman, were appointed to be heads of respectively BNP, Elf and UAP, thus underlining the view that the government still considers these to be strategic groups, even after privatization, and even though Jaffré and Friedman have no experience whatsoever in the industries to which they have been appointed.

The real clue to the extent to which government and business are closely interlocked in France is to be found in the role played by the **Ecole Nationale d'Administration** (ENA) in providing the **grands corps** of key servants of the state, service of which is 'noble' and transcends all else in life. But such servants serve business too, as they are parachuted from government ministries into top posts in the business world. Hence the decision-making élite of leading politicians and corporate bosses in both the state and private sector have been cast in the same mould and, in spite of ideological differences and party politics, share a common vision of the directions in which France should move. Patriotic *gloire* is not dead for this élite and they, more than any other factor, contribute most to the dirigiste model of France (see also Chapter 8 on management education).

Conclusion

The two presidencies of François Mitterand (1981–88, 1988–95) oversaw major shifts in economic and industrial policy which have entailed a fundamental sea-change for business. After the suicidal demand-led policies of the early 1980s and an increase in state intervention via a heady round of nationalizations, the emphasis since the mid-1980s has been on austere economic measures, a strong currency and supply-side changes, particularly on the labour-market front, although the effect on unemployment has been disappointing. Deregulation and privatization are now seen not only as essential but desirable by many in business as France has become rapidly enmeshed in globalization of business and the European Single Market. More than any other factors, however, the acceptability and legitimacy of business and profit-making have created a closer understanding between companies and French society.

Three issues loomed which are likely to dominate the relationship between government and business. First, the presidential elections in March 1995 produced a right-wing candidate although the Socialist candidate brought the Socialist party back from the dead with a strong showing. With Chirac as president, political considerations may well take over from smooth technocratic management and the *franc fort* policy challenged in a popular appeal to solve unemployment through devaluation and interest rate cuts. His prime minister, Alain Juppé, is staunchly pro-European, however, and is likely to restrain any attempt to divert France from Monetary Union, now billed for 1999.

Chirac will have to contend with the other two issues, the increasing corruption of leading political figures, a failing of both right and left, and the right balance to be struck between social provision and industrial competitiveness. More serious cases of corruption will not only further tarnish the image of politicians, already at a low ebb, but could well lead to an Italian-style purge. More seriously for business, the love affair between society and companies may grow rapidly cold as the workforce become disillusioned and angered with the business establishment. High levels of unemployment will further add to this mood. On the social provision front, the overriding challenge for a new president will be how to improve both competitiveness and employment prospects by relieving the burden of companies' contribution to the social security system yet at the same time satisfying the French workforce's claims for continuing protection of their featherbed of social privileges and advantages.

2 Business and the economy

Openness of the French economy

In terms of direct inward investment (using the Banque de France's definition of any investment in more than 10 per cent of a company), the French economy has never been so open. Indeed, it is so open that with job losses at their height, the level of xenophobia, to some extent always latent in France, is increasing as the global patterns of investment, ownership and employment bring the reality of mergers, acquisitions and relocations into the lives of ordinary Frenchmen and Frenchwomen.

In January 1993, Hoover closed its factory in Dijon and transferred production to Scotland. There were loud complaints of 'social dumping', of multinationals seeking the lowest wages, social costs, the most advantageous grants, and making their investment plans accordingly, thereby aggravating unemployment. In the same year, the South Korean manufacturers Daewoo set up a plant in Lorraine for the production of microwave ovens. This, too, brought howls of protest, this time from French industry which feared heightened competition and, again, the spectre of unemployment was invoked. A government report (the Arthuis report) on the relocation abroad of industry caused another stir over a phenomenon which, whilst not new in France, still came as a revolution in public eyes. In September 1993, the American company Lambert bought out the French producer of cachew nuts, Lajeunic, much to the consternation of the local population in Toulouse. It was consequently publicized that other household names in food products such as the Bêtises de Cambrai, the Galettes de Pleyben and Choco BN were no longer in French hands, but were owned by foreigners. In the opposite direction, Michelin took over Uniroyal in the United States, and Clermont Ferrand, where Michelin has its main production sites and headquarters, cried foul over job losses.

All these events underline the fundamental shift which has occurred, albeit belatedly, in the French investment and employment scene which has moved from a position of national independence and ownership to one of global interdependence. For many in France, the pill is hard to swallow but the process which started under the Socialists, with their policy of competitive deflation in 1983 and with European deregulation, has borne fruit and France is vigorously adapting to the open seas of global competition.

Companies controlled by foreign capital already contribute one-third of French sales and exports. They employ one-quarter of the workforce. Whereas they are particularly strong in high-tech sectors, they are less important in services where they account for 8 per cent of employees and 10 per cent of sales and commerce (13 per cent of employees and 17 per cent of sales) but, here too, they are gaining ground rapidly. Nearly two-thirds of the turnover of the top thirty French groups is achieved abroad, less and less by direct exports (24 per cent) and more and more by direct investment in overseas plants (38 per cent) in which globally French industrial companies employ one-quarter of their workforce. The net overall effect is that, out of every 100 employees in 'French' industry working in companies employing more than 20 (excluding energy, agri-business, building and public works), 20 work abroad for a subsidiary of a French group and 20 in France for the subsidiary of a foreign company. Another 17.5 work in France but for exports, leaving only 42.5 'Franco-French' producing in France, for a French company, products which are destined purely for the French market. This figure compares with 54.3 per cent eleven years ago. According to a report of the 'Plan', at least one out of every two employees in French industry, either on national soil or abroad, sees his/her job depend directly on location decisions taken on a transnational basis.

French industry started considerably later than most other industrialized countries in the vast movement of global restructuring which, since the beginning of the 1980s, has caused transnational investments to increase three times faster than world trade. It has now caught up and indeed, in 1992, beat all records by becoming the main target in the world for direct inward investment (using the Banque de France's definition but excluding reinvested profits which are included in the figures of the UK and other countries). Some 84 bn Ffr were directly invested, putting it far ahead even of the US, in a year when such investment slowed in other countries. In terms of outward investment this figure was counterbalanced by 99.6 bn Ffr directly invested by French companies overseas, putting it behind the USA but ahead of Germany and Japan.

The popular reaction to these revelations in the country of 'cocorico' is understandable, particularly because no attempt has been made to explain the underlying reasons. Both the government and the Banque de France treat it as a sensitive subject, not knowing how to manage it in the media, partially because of the unreliability of the statistics but particularly because the benefits of such trends in an open economy are not fully clear. The statistical office, INSEE, confesses to only fragmentary knowledge of the contribution such investments make to growth, employment and regional development.

The starting point of France's dash to catch up came in 1985 when the Socialist government decided to lift controls on French companies' freedom to invest abroad and then in 1987 with the decision to be proactive and to attract foreign investment to France. This was not because there was the positive desire to do so but because the construction of the European Single Market was forcing France away from being a relatively closed economy in which greenfield sites were considered favourably but where there was deep hostility felt to the mergers and acquisitions so dear to the Anglo-Saxons and made on stock exchanges which smacked of speculation and short-term profit.

Not that this was the first time direct investment had been made in France. Both with American investment in the wake of the Marshall Aid Plan and European investment in the 1960s after the creation of the Common Market, France had witnessed waves of inward foreign capital.

After the first oil shock of 1974, it closed up again, with the introduction of exchange controls and thus thwarting French companies' international ambitions. Where there was inward investment, it was scrutinized under a microscope and subject to stringent prior authorization by the government. With the adoption of the *franc fort* policy and deregulation of the financial and monetary markets, since 1985 French companies have literally rushed abroad benefiting from the 1987–90 economic boom, improving margins and closing the gap with their overseas competitors. In the space of just a few years, French investment overseas multiplied by seven, going from 20 bn Ffr at the beginning of the 1980s to 147 bn in 1990.

Initially, France was unable to take advantage of the global wave of investment. Whilst French companies expanded abroad, foreign investors shunned France because of its 'nationalist' and 'socialist' image. This led to a situation close to panic in the government (the gap was still 100 bn Ffr in 1990; see Figure 2.1), which in 1987 introduced measures not just to attract investment, but also not to block foreign capital. Now only non-EU investments exceeding 50 m Ffr are subject to prior authorization and accepted if no negative response is received within one month. In practice, most are accepted – out of 2,200 requests received in 1991, only one was rejected, for reasons of national security. In 1990, the regional development agency DATAR (**Direction à l'Aménagement du Territoire et à l'Action Régionale**) opened prospecting offices in all European countries and within the Finance Ministry the DREE (**Direction des Relations Economiques Extérieures** – Overseas Economic Relations Department) was

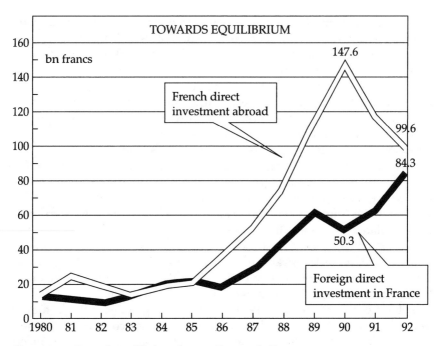

Figure 2.1   *Towards equilibrium. Source: Banque de France*

urged to court investors. In 1992, an **ambassadeur**, Jean Daniel Tordjman, was appointed to coordinate the whole of the French policy to attract inward investment.

The European Single Market is the principal driving factor as the government has belatedly accepted DATAR's long-standing argument that it was absurd not to take advantage of manna falling from a foreign heaven, particularly when overseas groups could set up elsewhere and gain direct access to the French market under Single Market rules. This was the period of animosity felt towards the UK government's policy of encouraging Japanese investment and led to its being labelled the Trojan Horse of Europe. France has now accepted the inevitable and has been, embarrassingly for its government, all too successful. Experts are still divided over the merits of such success but all are agreed now that it would be suicidal not to be part of the general movement, if only because Europe is where the majority of transnational investment is concentrated and shows no signs of abatement (it has been calculated that by the year 2000, foreign control of production could reach 50 per cent as opposed to 30 per cent in 1993).

In this aspect of industrial policy, however, the government is adopting a stance of some prudence. Aid will be forthcoming for 'national champions', particularly state companies, to invest abroad but not at the expense of French employment. Foreign investment will continue to be welcome but on condition that companies investing act as good citizens by bringing employment and new techniques, not by setting up screwdriver plants. Reciprocity is key to this watchful prudence, particularly as far as Japanese investment is concerned whose civic credentials, the French believe, still have to be proved in host countries.

Manufacturing

As in many other industrialized nations, with the exception of Japan and Germany, the relative economic importance of industry in France is declining in terms of added value and employment. Table 2.1 shows the relative contribution made to GDP by industry in selected countries between 1980 and 1990. In France, the drop was 3.4 per cent from 25.1 per cent in 1980 to 21.7 per cent. The situation in the UK has been more dramatic, industry's contribution falling by 6.1 per cent over the same period. In terms of industrial production, here too, France failed between 1980 and 1992 to achieve even the European average increase of 19 per cent, falling way below the OECD average of 127 (see Table 2.2) and being considerably outstripped by Germany, due principally to a chronic lack of investment until 1987. Whereas former West Germany's manufacturing investment increased between 1975 and 1987 by 44 per cent, France could only manage 14.3 per cent. There has been an accompanying fall in employment in industry (manufacturing industry, including agri-business and energy, but excluding construction, public works and transport) which now only accounts for 18 per cent (4.6 million employees), down from 25 per cent (5.6 million) twelve years ago (see Table 2.3). Only in the UK has a similar trend occurred, with much lower declines noticeable in both Germany and the USA and a remarkable 13 per cent growth in industrial employment in Japan.

In terms of the creation of new industrial companies, to compensate for the shakeout in employment in large industrial groups (–20 per cent, 1980–1990), new start-ups declined between 1980 and 1984, grew rapidly in 1985 and 1986, peaking at 21,000 but in spite of a boom period in the late 1980s, declined again, particularly after 1990. At the same time, the number of bankruptcies in industry has increased since 1980 at the annual rate of 14 per cent, making it the highest rate in Europe, some 60 per cent higher than the average for its industrial partners.

Although investment after 1987 grew rapidly, due to a dramatic improvement in companies' profitability, it has fallen since 1990 (see Table 2.4). Generally, however, the heads of large companies believe that industrial equipment is sufficient, in terms of age, quality and quantity, to cope

Table 2.1   *Share of industry in value-added (as % of GDP)*

	1980	1990	1990/80
France	25.1	21.7	−3.4
USA	21.8	18.7	−3.1
UK	27	20.9	−6.1
Germany	31.8	32.4	+0.6
Japan	27.9	29.2	+1.3

Source: OECD

Table 2.2   *Evolution of industrial production indices (base 100 in 1980)*

	1980	1985	1988	1989	1990	1991	1992
France	100	98	106	110	113	112	112
Germany	100	104	111	118	123	126	127
EC	100	103	112	116	119	119	119
USA	100	112	126	129	130	127	128
Japan	100	122	138	146	152	156	151
OECD	100	110	122	126	129	127	127

Source: OECD

Table 2.3   *Evolution of industrial employment*

	1980 (m)	1985 (m)	1988 (m)	1989 (m)	1990 (m)	% change 1990/80	1991 (m)	1992 (m)
France	5.63	5	4.69	4.70	4.72	−16	4.65	4.6
Germany	8.65	8.05	8.29	8.36	8.5	− 3	—	—
UK	6.17	5.32	5.16	5.15	5.1	−17	—	—
Italy	4.64	4.1	4.05	4.05	4.08	−12	—	—
USA	20.17	19.26	19.35	19.42	19.06	− 5	—	—
Japan	11.52	12.35	12.45	12.76	13.06	+13	—	—

Source: BIT, Geneva

with present and short-term demand. One major preoccupation of the 1980s, loss of industrial market share, now appears to be receding, the French economy in general and industry in particular having recovered half of the market share they lost between 1980 and 1985. Amongst the nine leading exporting nations, industrial market share has now regained the level achieved in 1970. The improvement has been most marked in

Table 2.4 *International comparisons of growth in productive investment*

	1980	1985	1988	1989	1990	1991
France	100	95.6	118.4	127.6	140.6	130.8
Germany	100	101.7	117.1	127.1	140.4	152.5
UK	100	131.4	182.4	197.2	195.1	171.8
USA	100	119.2	120.7	123.4	124.9	116.5
Japan	100	133.9	171.2	199.7	224.4	238.1

Source: OECD

the European Community, where its share of intra-community trade has increased more than that of its principal European trading partners, thus improving the spread of France's geographical exports, away from developing countries and more towards the developed, industrialized countries, a constant weakness often noted in French trade.

The Raynaud report of 1993 identified the newfound strengths of French manufacturing industry as follows.

1 Its greater internationalization (see above on investment), although more through relocation of overseas investment than through increase in exports. For companies in the 1–35 bn Ffr turnover range, the percentage of turnover achieved outside France went from 48 per cent in 1988 to 55 per cent in 1992, production in France dropped from 33 per cent to 31 per cent over the same period, and overseas production increased from 18 per cent to 24 per cent.
2 A better national economic environment. Corporation tax fell from 50 per cent to 42 per cent in 1988 and now stands at 34 per cent, which compares favourably with its European partners. In addition, the increase in real salaries has been very low in industry (less than 1 per cent annually between 1985 and 1991). Hourly costs, in spite of high social costs, are relatively competitive, although devaluations in the UK, Spain and Italy have jeopardized this competitiveness.
3 Debt levels, a traditional structural handicap, have declined as improved profit margins have allowed companies to repay debt. The level still remains higher than that in Germany, however.
4 Equity, in its scarcity once considered to be one of the major structural handicaps, has increased dramatically, particularly for large and medium-size companies. Thus equity represented on average 30 per cent of the balance sheet in 1991, as opposed to 27 per cent in 1988 and 20 per cent at the beginning of the 1980s.

As for weaknesses in industry, the report highlighted the following concerns.

Table 2.5   *R&D expenditure*

	Domestic expenditure on R&D (base 100: France 1980)			As % GDP		High-tech products market share (%)
	1980	*1990*	*1990/80*	*1980*	*1990*	
France	100	208	2.1	1.8	2.4	6.5
Germany	145	283	2	2.4	2.9	12
UK	107	176	1.6	2.25	2.3	7.7
USA	644	1305	2	2.3	2.8	20
Japan	204	550	2.7	2	3	17

Source: Raynaud Report

1   The comparative lack of companies employing between 1,000 and 2,000 employees, i.e. the German *Mittelstand* which has long been the envy of the French authorities. According to the Raynaud report, there are too few independent, family-owned, medium-sized companies and, where they do exist, they are mainly the subsidiaries of large groups. During the 1980s, over one-quarter of family firms lost control to larger groups. In 1980, 25 per cent of the total workforce were employed in small and medium-sized companies (**PMI – petites et moyennes industries,** also called **PME – petites et moyennes entreprises**) owned by groups; this figure had increased to 35 per cent in 1990 (also see Chapter 9).
2   Generally speaking, French companies invest less in research than their foreign competitors. As in most other countries, some 1.1 per cent of GDP is spent on public research, leaving 1.3 per cent spent by companies, compared with 1.7–1.8 per cent in Germany, the USA and Japan. In concrete terms, this translates into a weakness in high-tech product markets (Table 2.5). Industrial research is concentrated in just a few large sectors and in the largest companies. Six sectors account for three-quarters of R&D expenditure whereas these sectors only contribute one-third of industry's added value (electronics, aeronautics, automotive, chemicals, pharmaceuticals and energy). In addition, three-quarters of public research is carried out in the military and civil aeronautics sectors. But apart from this lack of technological R&D investment, France suffers, too, from insufficient expenditure on 'intangible' investments such as software, publicity, training, patents etc. As a percentage of tangible investment, this has doubled from 20 to 40 per cent over the period 1980–90, but is nevertheless some way behind that of the UK, for example, especially in software and advertising expenditure.

3   Quality and the environment were two major concerns which ap-
    peared in the 1980s. Nearly all companies place quality at the top
    of the list of their major preoccupations but in reality this appears to
    be mere lip-service as only 45 per cent have undertaken any ser-
    ious form of quality activity, the notion of 'total quality' seeming less
    developed in France than in Japan, Germany and Northern Europe.
    In terms of companies certified for quality assurance systems, how-
    ever, the equivalent of BS 5750, France ranks in second position after
    the UK.

Many companies are undertaking 'environment' programmes (18 per
cent of total industrial investment), which, it is hoped, will bring French
industry up to North European standards although, generally speaking,
French industrialists have always considered the environment more as a
constraint than as a means of developing new products and technologies. Whereas 'green' labels have existed in Germany since 1977 covering a multitude of different products, the first such label, 'NF France',
appeared in 1992 under a voluntary pilot scheme introduced by AFNOR
(**Agence Française de Normalisation**) the French standard-setting body
and only applicable to paints.

'Green' products, without the backing of an official label, have existed
since the end of the 1980s but only account for a negligible 7 per cent of
sales. According to a Ministry of Industry survey, out of 8,000 companies in seventy-eight different sectors, only 14 per cent manufacture eco-
products. Few PME are involved, the majority of products being made by
the large industrial groups. The reality is that in France few consumers are
convinced by the environment argument in their daily purchases. They
fear big pollution disasters but rarely make the link between their daily
behaviour and the balance of nature. Inadequate information is one reason, as is their lack of willingness to pay more for eco-products which
have to prove their effectiveness. They must be innovative, cheaper and
as good to sell in France. But perhaps the most important factor is the
absence of a strong consumer movement in France capable of mobiliz-
ing consumers around green products, as in Anglo-Saxon countries.

Vehicle building

The automotive industry in many respects encapsulates the globalizing
trends affecting French industry and the resulting tension between argu-
ments calling for a certain level of protectionism, 'fair' trade rather than
free trade, resistance to relocation of industry outside France and those

which accept the inevitability of the upheaval caused by the growing interdependence of trading countries and the necessity to improve productivity to compete.

In 1991, PSA (Peugeot-Citroën) was the most profitable car company in the world, followed in 1992 by Renault with a net profit of 5.7 bn Ffr, an increase of 8.1 per cent in spite of three years of decline in the European market. The success of these two companies, both amongst the top ten companies in France, was the culmination of ten years' restructuring and modernization, ahead of the Americans and other European manufacturers, during which 121,000 jobs disappeared (30 per cent of employees) but production increased by 30 per cent. According to both companies, there are a number of reasons for this success.

First, the domestic market is still protected for some years to come from Japanese imports, both directly from Japan and those from Japanese-owned plants in the USA. Transplants made in the United Kingdom are also still subject to annual progressive ceilings. The industry pleaded for and won respite to bring productivity up to Japanese car manufacturers' level before an entirely free market is allowed. Hence the battle is on to reduce costs by 15 per cent over three years, resulting in fierce negotiation with reluctant sub-contractors to compress prices and in a move to improve distribution networks and after-sales service. In spite of restrictions on transplants, they pose a growing major threat, however, as do Rover after the devaluation of the British currency, but other devaluations also led to heightened competition from Ford, Fiat and Seat. The strong franc is thus posing the biggest danger to the French car manufacturers' combined domestic market share of 62.3 per cent (Renault 29.5 per cent, Peugeot 19.4 per cent, Citroën 13.4 per cent) although helped in 1994 by a government subsidy of 5,000 Ffr to those buying a new car in exchange for scrapping an old car over ten years old. Time has been bought, then, for a flagship industry which plays such a vital part in the economy and which believes in an orderly restructuring and reconfiguration of markets rather than a potentially destructive free-for-all. Renault's future status underlies this with the government's plans for its privatization, stressing the company's technological, social – it pioneered many labour relations provisions – and political importance. In its final plans for privatization in late 1994, the government retained absolute control with 51 per cent of its shares.

Secondly, modernized plant has contributed to the industry's success but here the French companies have adopted solutions which have broken with the growing belief in 'lean' production methods as practised by the Japanese car manufacturers. Renault, in particular, is no believer in 'lean' production since although it is highly flexible, it involves dramatically higher equipment costs (+30–40 per cent). The diversity of models it affords is an advantage in expanding markets but becomes too big a burden when markets contract. Below 3 per cent market growth, diversity is pointless; above 7 per cent Renault believes mass production is still the most profitable and has invested accordingly for the production of its Twingo. At Peugeot, too, automation is seen as necessary but not to excess, and they point to the problems at Fiat caused by too heavy investment.

Thirdly, the choice of alliances has been crucial, which in the case of PSA, with the merging of Peugeot and Citroën, has led to common parts being used, common logistics and finance, etc. At Renault, much hope had been pinned on the defunct merger with Volvo and there is little doubt that a new partner (Fiat has been mooted as a possibility) will be actively sought in an industry where companies need critical size to survive the necessity to invest in new models.

Fourthly, Renault and PSA are comparatively unintegrated. In contrast to Fiat and the Japanese manufacturers where sub-contractors are often part of the group, they use more external suppliers, to the extent that purchases represent 65 per cent of the cost of a car. This, they believe, has helped to reduce costs and afforded a higher level of flexibility, albeit not always to the benefit of the sub-contractors.

Lastly, the product strategy, although debatable with Peugeot's heavy backing of the diesel option, has with Renault's range from the Twingo to the Safrane, via the Clio and the R19, brought increasing acclaim for its breadth and quality. Increased exports have followed, particularly to Germany.

If the car manufacturers' strategy exemplifies the cautious, protectionist model, the car equipment manufacturer, Valeo, belongs very firmly in the free trade and competitive open market camp. Number one in France, number two in Europe behind the German company Bosch, in 1992 it increased investment by 36 per cent, at the same time reducing its 26,000-strong workforce. It has built four new factories, one each in France, Wales, Italy and Brazil, thus continuing the drive for greater internationalization commenced in 1987. Exports account for 66 per cent of turnover (17 per cent in America and Asia) and GM voted the company its top suppplier in 1993. It supplies parts to all the major car manufacturers, in particular to the American and European factories of the Japanese manufacturers (forecast to represent 10 per cent of turnover by 1996), thus underlining the paradoxical nature of French resistance to Japanese investment in Europe. Even more significantly, it has been less affected by devaluation, causing problems for Renault and Peugeot since it simply switched production to lower cost plants elsewhere in the world, thereby causing anger over job losses in France and amongst its French suppliers from whom it sought a 3 per cent price reduction.

The notion of industrial policy with the state playing a pivotal role is unashamedly and positively embraced in France and no more so than in the automotive industry where a dogmatic and heavily interventionist approach is giving way to a more pragmatic *realpolitik*. The state presses for an overall strategic framework which limits damage, using its increasingly more limited powers of ownership to positive effect and leaving the industry itself to cope with competitive conditions. Thus Peugeot can take advantage of the state's protection of Renault but Valeo has no alternative but to connive with the reality of Japanese transplants.

The defence industry

The sector as a whole represents one of the stars of the French economy (number three in the world, number one in Europe in terms of turnover and exports), with a turnover of 116 bn Ffr of which 25 per cent comes from exports. With the exception of Matra, Europe's leading missile manufacturer, it remains firmly in state hands (Thomson, Aérospatiale, SNECMA, Dassault, GIAT industries and nine other arms manufacturers including naval dockyards). As elsewhere, it has suffered from a combination of recession and the so-called 'peace dividend', although France, in 1994, was the only large Western country to increase its defence budget, which represents some 3.4 per cent of GDP (UK 3.2 per cent, Germany 2.2 per cent, Italy 2 per cent, Spain 1.7 per cent). In 1993, it obtained a particular boost in difficult markets with the sale of 390 Leclerc tanks by GIAT to the United Arab Emirates (the first order outside France where the army scaled down its initial order from 1,200 to 650) and 60 Mirage 2,000–5 fighters to Taiwan, thus maintaining the 1992 level of exports of French military equipment (already up by 46 per cent on 1991). In spite of this success, however, more job losses are feared in an overmanned industry which now employs directly and indirectly 400,000 as opposed to 700,000 ten years ago.

Losses of some 60,000 direct jobs and 40,000 indirect jobs are forecast up to 1995, unless the government extends its moratorium on redundancies in state-owned industries announced in September 1993. But the sector includes some 5,000 PME for whom there will be little respite, particularly as more and more countries repatriate sub-contracts to national manufacturers.

Again, the presence of a large state-owned sector illustrates the limitations of France's nationalization policy and the consequent flexible solutions being sought in an area where privatization is not on the agenda. First, under-capitalization of some state companies is of major concern at a time when self-generated funds, the result of government cut-backs, are increasingly the order of the day. Partnerships and restructuring are therefore the major priorities, both in France and elsewhere, as everyone discusses with everyone – in the USA, between West and East Europe and between Europe and South-East Asia. The overall concern is to pool potential markets, research and development and technical resources and manpower which are no longer within the power of any one company or nation to finance. Nationalized status, however, is hampering both Thomson and Aérospatiale in the USA where they are forbidden to own American companies. This raises the interesting question of the French government's attitude to foreign investment in these companies, if privatization eventually materializes. At the very least, it is unlikely, given the present American attitude and even assuming this changes with privatization, that American investment will be allowed in a sector contributing to national security and independence in defence.

Secondly, the status of GIAT has been changed from that of **régie** – under direct government administration – to that of **société nationale**, which will allow it the freedom to export without passing through state intermediaries. With shrinking or stable national defence budgets, exports are key to the future of the French defence industry and to some extent explain France's eagerness to replace both the USA and the UK as gendarme in the world's trouble spots. In Cambodia (part of Indochina, a former French colony), in the former Yugoslavia, and in Africa (Rwanda, Zaire) France, with or without the UN, is eagerly pursuing a policy of engaging in overseas action to fill the vacuum left by the Cold War. Its motives are partially and laudably humanitarian, but there is little doubt, particularly in Africa, where it still has major interests, that France's action can be explained by more calculatedly pragmatic reasons, including the promotion of its defence industry.

Luxury goods

Perfumes, bags, scarves from companies such as L'Oréal, Yves St-Laurent, Hermès, Vuitton – for many, these are the traditional image of France at its best and certainly recent results and trends underline French strength. With the explosion of sales worldwide, turnover in the sector in France increased by 18 per cent in 1988, with value added standing at 40 per cent of turnover and gross trading profits at 13 per cent. In 1988, luxury goods as a whole (including château-bottled wine) showed a positive trade balance of 36 bn Ffr, considerably more than the 25 bn Ffr for military equipment. When Yves St-Laurent sought a listing on the Paris stock exchange, it had to be delayed because the issue was oversubscribed some 260 times! Indeed, the wheel went full circle: French ministers once considered that modern France had much more serious things to offer than perfume and wine but became so alarmed at seeing the jewels of the French luxury industry falling into foreign hands that they initially blocked Japanese attempts to buy into the distribution of the exclusive Romanée Conti wine. But the nature of the industry has changed, moving to a blend of high-tech processes and traditional craft skills with companies generally preferring to re-invest profits than distribute dividends. It is also breeding a new generation of managers, typified by Bernard Arnault, the mercurial head of LVMH (Louis–Vuitton–Moët–Henessy), which is ousting the old family owners and replacing maintenance of traditions with more emphasis on modern management techniques and profitability.

But coinciding with the Gulf War, storm clouds began to appear on the clear horizon of the French luxury goods industry. Recession in the USA and the fall in the value of yen were just two of the more obvious causes. More fundamental was increasing competition, from the USA and particularly from their own backyard, Italy. Already, France's share of the world luxury goods market had fallen from 75 per cent in 1975 to 50 per cent in 1989. France's leadership is still impressive but Italian brands in sectors such as food, jewellery, haute couture and luxury off-the-peg clothing are achieving superior growth rates. Even French fine wines are not spared: chemical contamination scares, drink-and-driving campaigns, competition from Californian and Australian wines, and from branded spirits, have all seriously dented France's supremacy.

Hermès has weathered the recession particularly well and was introduced to the Bourse (stock exchange) in 1993. Turnover increased by 16 per cent and after-tax profit by 19 per cent. Silk and leather products, plus ready-to-wear clothes, accounted for the major increases and the company intends expanding its boutiques in airports. LVMH, on the other hand, has suffered badly from the crisis in the champagne industry which has been particularly affected by the recession in Europe which accounts for three-quarters of sales. The most prestigious labels, such as Moët et Chandon have been hardest hit with LVMH's market share dropping from 21 per cent to 19 per cent. Its perfume and luggage activities continue to hold up well, however – another example of the French traditional luxury industry bucking the trend.

Services

Two major structural factors are generating unemployment in France: the tertiarization of industry and the industrialization of services. Old jobs are being profoundly changed in industry as computers are used more and more at the heart of production. As cadres and technicians have taken over from production workers so productivity has made big gains but at the expense of making the least qualified redundant. The phenomenon is increasing as competition from low-wage countries and saturation of markets leads to added value being sought in quality and particularly customer service. As for services, greater productivity is arising from the use of new technologies and being accelerated by the recession, particularly in services to companies, personal services, banking and property. There was a halt in the rise of new jobs in services in 1990, while 1991 saw a decline, with an increase in bankruptcies leading to rationalization and ensuing staff reductions. The whole trend is underpinned by the 'productivity' philosophy which seems more pronounced in France than in other countries and could have the same effect as in industry, with unemployment eliminating low qualifications.

In 1993, services accounted for 69.8 per cent of GDP and 66.1 per cent of employment. The biggest boom in services occurred in the 1980s, growing in value by 232 per cent between 1980 and 1981. One million new jobs were created, whereas agriculture lost 612,000 and industry 1,240,000 jobs. In commercial services (**services marchands**, i.e. non-government) the largest companies include Publicis (advertising), ECCO (employment agency), CAP Gemini-Sogeti (computer services), ACCOR (the world's largest hotel group including the Sofitel, Novotel and Ibis chains), Club Méditerranée (tour operator) and Générale des Eaux (a water company specializing in services to local councils and cable television), banks and insurance.

The era of growth of *services marchands* ended in 1991 with a small rise in unemployment and a particularly big drop in services to companies as recession began to take hold in industry (see Table 2.6). Some 215,000 redundancies were recorded in 1991 and 249,000 in 1992, almost as many as in industry. Pressure on prices was undoubtedly a major factor in the 18 per cent increase in bankruptcies, as too was the trend towards companies 'repatriating' services such as recruitment to their own in-house departments. Although the job losses did not quite match those in industry, the situation could have been far worse if some companies had not delayed some cuts for fear of an **explosion sociale**, a much-heard phrase in France as the unemployment figures worsen.

Although services still operate within a relatively protected environment in France with little international competition, the possibility of relocation via teleworking, i.e. accounting being performed in South East Asia, underlines a growing threat. Whereas inward investment now accounts for 28 per cent in industry, the figure stands at 10 per cent for services. But foreign direct investment in services in France has more than doubled in recent years, with French investments abroad lagging worryingly some way behind.

Table 2.6   *Breakdown of employment by sector*

Sector	No. employed*		Value added*	
	1980	*1991*	*1980*	*1991*
Agriculture	8.6	5.7	4.5	3.2
Industry	34.3	28.2	35.5	29.9
Tertiary	57.1	66.1	60.0	66.9
Non-commercial services	21.9	25.4	16.8	16.5
Commercial services	35.2	40.7	43.2	50.4
Commerce	12.1	12.3	10.9	11.1
Transports	3.5	3.9	4.2	3.9
Telecommunications	1.9	2.0	2.0	2.1
Insurance and finance	2.6	2.7	4.6	4.4
Property services	—	—	6.8	8.9
Other commercial services:	15.1	19.8	14.7	20.0
Services to companies	5.9	8.5	6.7	9.6
Services to individuals	4.6	5.9	4.3	5.6
Hotels, cafes, restaurants	2.7	3.6	2.1	3.0
Vehicle repairs	1.9	1.8	1.6	1.8
Total†	21,847,100	22,204,500	2,667,572	6,505,029

* Percentage of total.
† Millions of francs (for the value added).
Source: INSEE

In terms of contribution to the balance of payments, traditionally services have made up for the deficit on industrial goods, as France continues to be the world's biggest exporter of services after the USA. The surplus in 1991 was 50.1 bn Ffr, although much of this was due to tourism, which alone contributed France's largest balance of payments surplus of 51 bn. France continues to be the most popular country in the world for tourists, attracting some 60 billion annually, who represent 36 per cent of hotel clients, a third of camp site bookings, 52 per cent of the department stores' turnover and 70 per cent of the luxury goods industry turnover. The French themselves largely spend their holidays at home, only 16 per cent going abroad, as against 33 per cent for the rest of Europe. In spite of the cultural backlash created by Euro Disney, dubbed a 'cultural Chernobyl', it is the number one tourist attraction for the French, after Notre Dame, the Louvre and the Eiffel Tower. Outside of Paris, the palace of Versailles, Lourdes and Mont Saint-Michel are the most popular sites. Of those going abroad, only 3 million take package tours as against 10 million in Germany and the United Kingdom. The top four national tour operators – of which there are over 200 – in a highly fragmented market, only account for 29 per cent of total demand as against 80 per cent in Germany. Thus, lacking the commercial clout of the big vertically integrated German and British tour operators, Touropa of France, for example, charges 73 per cent more than Thomson in the United Kingdom for the same holiday, half-board in the same hotel in Benidorm in Spain.

Much has been said in France about the productivity philosophy having too high a social cost without any automatic improvement in quality. A government report cited the case of no more petrol-pump attendants meaning no more checking of oil and water levels and no washing of windscreens! There is some considerable debate about re-employing more people in these traditional services but with greater enrichment of work content, as in the USA and Japan (where productivity in services is very low), for example, where qualified consumer assistants give advice in department stores. Such a move would need highly unlikely concertation between employers, however, as no one company would want to be penalized by taking the first step.

Growth has been particularly spectacular in the retail sector, where concentration has been the most prominent feature, with the rise of Europe's largest retailer, Carrefour and other groups such as Casino, Auchan and Mammouth. Yet, in spite of the presence of 970 hypermarkets, 450 of which are more than 7,000 m², the retail sector still remains more fragmented than in the United Kingdom. No one group has more than 5 per cent market share and the top forty groups account for only 37 per cent of the retail trade's total turnover. Independent retailers as a whole still account for 46 per cent of retail distribution as opposed to 25 per cent in the United Kingdom, thus underlining the fact that whereas in the United Kingdom the chief buyers of the top twelve major chains need to be persuaded to buy a product before it appears on shelves from Lands End to John O'Groats, in France even contacting all of the top purchasing organizations will not ensure that a product will reach the twenty-five largest centres of population.

It is a sector, too, where there is very little sense of mutually beneficial cooperation between manufacturers and retailers. Relations are on more of an open-war footing – as are relations between retailers – as price margins are pared to the bone in a highly competitive sector where consumers discriminate fiercely on price only, the result of stagnating wages in a low-inflation economy which finally ran out of steam in 1992–3 with the drop in exports to reunified Germany. The retailers have the edge on manufacturers, who increasingly point to demands for impossible price cuts as a major cause of job losses and greater penetration of cheaper imported goods. Suppliers' representatives are virtually broken on the rack by buying organizations (**centrales d'achat**), particularly of the fiercely independent Intermarché chain (many of the largest retailers have no equity) where shops are bought on a franchise basis and owners, therefore, have often their life savings at stake. Manufacturers pay huge sums not to be delisted, are forced to pay for promotion campaigns and often for shop extensions. France, too, is the only country in Europe where **refus de vente** (refusal to sell) is illegal and hence retailers are at complete liberty – using the delisting threat – to cut prices, particularly through the use of loss-leaders on consumer electronics goods. In its drive to contain inflationary measures, the government was once not displeased to see low prices, but is now in an anti-competitive and anti-free-trade mood, alarmed that manufacturers are being so squeezed that the retail trade is cited as a prime cause of French industry's problems and of its consequent relocations abroad (Arthuis report). Profits are consequently low: for the same turnover as Carrefour, Marks and Spencer makes seven times more profit (although profits may be understated in France, accounts being prepared only for the tax authorities). The average profit margin can be as low as 1 to 1.5 per cent, with as much as 80 per cent of this profit margin deriving from managing the cash flow. On average, hypermarket stock rotates once every twenty-four days, while sixty days are normally taken to pay suppliers, thus providing thirty-six days of cash to invest. Unofficially, however, it is not uncommon to find certain hypermarket chains, particularly the independents, taking up to 110 days to pay suppliers.

The **Loi Royer** of 1973 established regional commissions to regulate the building of new hypermarkets and, as a result, the commission being heavily weighted in favour of local small retailers, a firm brake was put on any extension to the market. This led most major groups to set up abroad with no fewer than 100 French hypermarkets to be found as far apart as Brazil (15) and Spain (53). French hypermarket chains have indeed excelled precisely in countries with a highly fragmented distribution system, but on the whole failed in the more concentrated systems of Northern Europe (e.g. the United Kingdom).

An increasing threat to French retailers are the 'hard discounters' selling a restricted number of popular lines (**les premiers prix**). Most are German, with one a day opening in France. In 1991 there were 640 – in September 1992 there were 1,016 with a turnover of 25 bn Ffr. French retailers have reacted by opening similar stores, as they increasingly attract not only blue- and white-collar workers but also one in two *cadres*. Although hypermarkets are worried, who with their low margins consider their prices unbeatable, they continue to fare well, turning in the best increase in sales in the first half of 1993. The biggest effect is on the small and medium-size local stores such as supermarkets and superettes and on the lower-priced department stores in town centres (**les magasins populaires**), such as Monoprix and Prisunic, already badly hit by the hypermarkets.

One big factor in the uncontrolled rise of the discounters is that they can grow without restraint because they are unaffected by the Loi Royer.

In the retail textile and clothing sector the mail-order houses (**VPC – vente par correspondance**) continue to mystify experts with their unchecked growth, even without the advantage of discounts. The most common explanation put forward is that their customers prefer to stay put in their own region in a country where the population density is half that of the United Kingdom. The up-market stores (**les grands magasins**), however, are going through a lean time with inflexible structures preventing them from reacting quickly to market changes and caught between the temptation to reduce prices and the desire to differentiate through quality of service, more luxurious surroundings etc. One new phenomenon on the retail scene is the emergence of the **Maxi-livres** book-selling chain which offers discounts on books more than one year old, as allowed by the **Loi Lang**.

Finally in the retail sector, as elsewhere, big battles are being waged between own labels (**marque de distributeur**) and brands as consumers seek ever lower prices. Again, own labels are blamed for job losses as they limit retailers' and suppliers' margins and increase imports. There is the feeling in France that although the brand hype had become excessive, nevertheless, brands had created employment for a whole group of people in services.

One other service sector of some interest, in that it provides an insight into government attitudes towards so-called 'strategic' sectors of national importance, is that of newspapers. Almost without exception, although they have never, particularly at national level, been as strong as in other countries, particularly the UK, they are haemorrhaging financially. In addition, they are hampered by the **livre** section of the CGT which enjoys a *de facto* closed shop and vigorously opposes any whiff of change, particularly if it involves the use of modern, non-unionized plant. Two new laws, the **Loi Evin** and the **Loi Sapin** respectively banning cigarette and alcohol advertising, have provided a final nail in their coffin. The state responded by providing a subsidy of 200 million francs over the 1993–4 period and a pledge to allocate a quota of the publicity for new privatization issues to the press. Employing 56,000 directly and 200,000 indirectly with a turnover of 56 bn Ffr it has been described by the government as *'le baromètre de notre démocratie'*, although by no means as virulent and brutal as much of the Anglo-Saxon press. Of great interest, too, has been the decision by Pierre Suard, the former head of Alcatel–Alsthom, the world's second largest telecommunications equipment manufacturer and also maker of the TGV and major electricity generating plant, to diversify into publishing. Already owners of 100 per cent of the Express group and 24.3 per cent of CEP Communication, the largest professional publishing group, its publishing subsidiary Générale Occidentale (GO) acquired in

1993 40 per cent of the weekly magazine *Le Point*. The quite unashamedly announced motive was to block the entry of foreign groups into the French press. Suard, one of the most powerful figures in the French business establishment, is known, however, for his irritation at comments made in the press and this, together with the protectionist stance, points to the conclusion that there may be some level of covert control exercised by the government and the establishment over the business press which is not lightly to be relinquished.

Conclusion

As in other major industrialized countries, France has had to come to terms with three major transformations over the past fifteen years: growing globalization of markets and internationalization of its firms, the growth of service industries and a concomitant level of deindustrialization and the rise of the small firms.

As has been seen, France gives the lie to the oft-held perception that it is highly protectionist by displaying an openness to direct foreign investment which has drastically increased over the past seven to eight years. At the same time, French businesses have sought investment abroad, either through mergers and acquisitions or through relocation of manufacturing in their awareness of the interdependence of economies and the necessity to become globally competitive. Responsibility for levels of unemployment hitherto unseen in France has, however, been laid at the door of internationalizing industry and cries have been heard for greater protection.

Service industries have been seen as the white-hot hope of employment as they swiftly took on the mantle of the major providers of jobs. As industry has tertiarized, services have become industrialized and with this trend, unemployment has struck the service sector, too. In the case of both industry and services, then, change has brought much pain and, as was seen in Chapter 1, the major challenge of the president will be to engineer an economy flexible enough, particularly in its labour market, to respond more robustly and swiftly. The third transformation has been the rise of the small firm and it is here that increasing interest will be shown since, in spite of a draconian number of failures, those companies which have consistently won through in the French economy have been dynamic, family-owned small and medium-size companies, particularly in the old traditional sectors of food and drink, luxury goods and retail distribution according to a study by the 'Association pour le développement de l'histoire économique'.

Although a number of large companies have succeeded well, there is a view that France is relatively less good at producing standardized goods in large companies run by managers who have often emerged from the civil service, understand markets less well, therefore, and view the state as a guardian angel. If profit is taken as the main criterion, over the long term, the French PME have outscored large companies throughout the twentieth century. *La crise* has only reinforced Ricardo's theory of competitive advantage when applied to France and led to the belief spelt out in the Raynaud report that the country needs more family-owned medium-size companies.

3 Business and the law

Introduction

In a country like France with a civil law system based on Roman law and with substantial reliance on codified law, it is surprising to discover that French law has not yet found a satisfactory definition for the term 'business', or more correctly, **fonds de commerce**. Definitions abound, as we shall discover, of the nature and purpose of different company forms of doing business but nothing formalized exists to explain precisely what a *fonds de commerce* really is. In fact, a business in French legal parlance is principally defined by an identifiable customer base. This is what people lose or acquire when they sell or buy a business in France. They may choose to include or not in the deal physical or tangible assets. This means that any building, plant or goods etc. has to be explicitly noted in the contract of sale otherwise it is not assumed to be an integral and transferable part of the business. Ownership of a *fonds de commerce* does not itself mean ownership of property or, indeed, contractual rights.

Company structure and purpose

The most common forms of company in France are: the **Société Anonyme**, the **Société à Responsabilité Limitée**, the **Société en Nom Collectif**, the **Société en Commandite Simple** (although less common now), the **Société en Commandite par Actions**, the **Groupement d'Intérêt Economique** and the **Société en Participation**. Other forms of company do exist in the financial and property investment sectors as well as in regional development but this section will focus on the principal corporate vehicles for undertaking business. A company cannot be bought 'off the shelf' in France as an association of people is required to exploit a *fonds de commerce* for which premises are needed.

The Société Anonyme (SA)

The SA must have a minimum of seven shareholders whose liability is limited to their contribution to the share capital of the enterprise. There are no restrictions on the nationality of shareholders nor whether they are private or corporate entities. A distinction between private and quoted SAs is that the former requires a minimum share capital of 250,000 Ffr whereas a quoted company must have at least 1,500,000 Ffr in capital. If a shareholder wishes to contribute 'in-kind' to the establishing of an SA then the shares contributed in this way need to be paid up at the time of issue. However, if the share contribution is in cash then only 25 per cent must be paid at the time of issue with the remainder paid on request by the board of directors within a five-year period from the date of their issue.

This initial capital of the company has to be deposited with a bank or similarly authorized institution at the same time as the company's Articles of Association signed by the shareholder. The board and chairman are then appointed and the constitution of the company has to be published in the *Bulletin des Annonces Légales et Obligatoires*. Once certified, the name of the company has to be filed with the clerk of the Commercial Court (**Tribunal de Commerce**), entered on the Commercial Register and a company registration number issued. When the appropriate declarations have been made to the tax (including a fixed payment of 500 Ffr) and social security authorities and all necessary fees paid, the company can start trading, but not before another announcement of its existence, this time in the *Bulletin Officiel des Annonces Civiles et Commerciales (BODACC)*.

An SA can be structured in two ways: either by having a **conseil d'administration** (board of directors) and a **président** (chairman of the board) or a two-level management structure which has an operational board of directors (**directoire**) reporting to a supervisory board (**conseil de surveillance**).

The number of members of an SA board of directors can be between three and fifteen (twelve for a private listed SA). Again, there are not any restrictions on nationality or legal identity for membership of a board. Non-EU citizens need to obtain a so-called commercial card (**carte commerciale**), however, which may take up to 6–8 months to obtain. The *président* of the board can be voted off the board by a single majority of the directors. Often, up to two general managers are appointed to assist the *président* in running the company and this team has full authority to commit the company in commercial transactions without necessarily informing the whole board. General meetings of shareholders have virtually no teeth and the board is only formally answerable to its shareholders. In their turn members of the board are only there to back up the chairman. Some have called it management by divine right, with chairmen not answerable to anyone – votes are rare and, indeed, if a proposal is put to the vote, it is seen virtually as a sign of no confidence in the chairman and time for him to resign.

Heads of both state and private companies often have numerous places on different boards of directors and between them symbolize the concentration of power which is characteristic of large French companies and make many of them bid-proof. By law no more than eight seats on different boards may be held by any one person, but in reality many get round this by representing people who do officially have a seat. The inevitable result in many cases is only scant knowledge of the detailed workings of a company's business and hence greater reliance on the authority of the chairman. Absenteeism is rife, as in French law there is no obligation to mention attendance at board meetings in annual reports. The notion of working committees is also virtually unknown, and board members are very rarely taken to court for negligence. Add to this the fact that in both private and state companies, the main decisions are not taken during board meetings, but as a result of discussion between a few key board members, and the picture of the extensive cross-linking powers of board chairman is complete.

In the case of a 'dual management' structured SA, the directorate (between two and seven members) have operational responsibility, with the supervisory board retaining executive authority. The supervisory board members (between three and twelve) are nominated by the shareholders. One of the ironies of the dual form of management is that members of a directorate can only be dismissed by a vote at a general meeting of shareholders and that, therefore, the supervisory board's 'executive power' is somewhat constrained in practice. Although the single tier SA is the most common form in France, the dual management structure is often preferred by foreign companies/shareholders wishing to establish French subsidiaries.

A government bill relating to unquoted SAs is currently being enacted which would give much greater freedom to privately capitalized companies in defining their articles of association and internal management structure. This new form of SA company (*Société par Actions*) would require only a minimum of two shareholders but share capital of 1,500,000 Ffr which would have to be fully paid at the time of issue.

The Société à Responsabilité Limitée (SARL)

An SARL can have between one and fifty shareholders. (If there is only one shareholder then the type of company is usually called an EURL – **Entreprise Unipersonnelle à Responsabilité Limitée**). With a minimum share capital value of 50,000 Ffr and each share worth at least 100 Ffr (paid up at time of issue), an SARL has to remain a private/unquoted company.

The management of an SARL is identified by the articles of association or by a shareholders' meeting. Normally, one or more **gérants** are appointed to run the company – there is no board of directors – and they, in turn, can choose to delegate specific responsibilities to one or more directors. An SARL *gérant* has legal liability for any action which is deemed to be in contravention of legislation relating to this form of company or for breaking the stated articles of association, or, indeed, any errors of judgement in managing the company. As *gérants* have the power to do anything, and their removal is difficult, it is common practice not to appoint them for a long period.

In the case of an SARL the structure is well suited to a medium-sized enterprise, being simpler in form and liability than an SA. There is, however, and literally, 'a price to be paid' for this simplicity. As opposed to an SA, an SARL's shares must be paid up on subscription and cannot be negotiated. In addition, any transfer of SARL shares is penalized by a registration tax of 4.8 per cent of the transaction value, which tends to discourage such transfers.

Officers of companies (chairman, general manager, managing director etc.) are all subject to civil liability for violations of the law and are personally liable for all sorts of mishaps (e.g. the collapse of the football stand in Bastia). There is no idea of corporate responsibility and personal liability is not insurable.

Both the SA and the SARL are what is known as **sociétés de capitaux** (limited liability of the shareholders and shareholder identity is not a critical factor in establishing the business). There are still, however, a vast number of very small and small-sized companies in France. According to some statistics there are nearly 700,000 commercial enterprises in France of which the overwhelming majority are extremely small in relative terms. In such businesses partnership plays an important role. These companies are known as **sociétés de personnes** and the identity of the partners is a crucial factor given that their liability is joint, several and unlimited.

The Société en Nom Collectif (SNC)

If two or more individuals decide to establish a partnership in business in France then they immediately assume the legal status of **commerçants** (traders) and as such become jointly and severally liable for any debts the company has, and, even more importantly, their liability is unlimited. An SNC does not require share capital nor do its shares need to be paid up at time of issue or within a fixed period. Transfers of shares to another partner or to an 'outsider' have to be agreed by all the partners unless explicitly allowed in the articles of association. Partners also decide when drafting the articles of association how profits and losses should be allocated. Profits and losses may be shared out in different ways among the partners and there is not, necessarily, any correlation between a partner's share in the profits and his/her share in the company's capital.

One cannot, however, make one partner eligible for receiving all profits or all losses.

Partners in an SNC have substantial flexibility in deciding how their business should be run. They also, in practice, often appoint a *gérant* to manage the company. In addition to this flexibility, SNCs are considered 'transparent' in terms of corporate taxation, with each of the partners liable to be taxed on that income which he/she receives from the company and in accordance with his/her current tax status. If one of the partners is itself a legal entity with limited liability then the disadvantages of unlimited liability as an integral part of SNC status is simply overcome. There still remains, however, a registration tax of 4.8 per cent of any shares transferred within the partnership.

The Société en Commandite Simple (SCS)

This form of company has a similar status to the SNC with no need for a minimum share capital sum or for shares to be paid up. The SCS has a 'dual management' structure similar to that described for an SA. However, in an SCS two sets of partners exist: first, one or more managing partners (called the **commandités**) who, just as in the case of an SNC, are jointly, severally liable and to an unlimited extent for any company losses and debts; secondly, one or more partners (called the **commanditaires**) whose role is solely to provide share capital to the businesses. The liability of the commanditaires is limited as long as they do not involve themselves in any active way in the day-to-day management of the business. Very few companies still have the status of Société en Commandite Simple.

Agreement is needed by both sets of partners for any transfer of shares to a third party to be undertaken, and a *gérant*, who can be one of the *commandités* but not a *commanditaire*, is usually appointed in a similar way to that noted in the case of an SNC.

An SCS, unlike an SNC, is liable for full corporate taxation and for this reason, as well as its more complex dual management structure, it is less popular than an SNC.

The Société en Commandite par Actions (SCA)

The SCA is a form of company structure which draws upon aspects of an SCS and aspects of an SA.

An SCA requires at least four shareholders with a minimum of three *commanditaires* and one *commandité*. It can be quoted publicly with a minimum public share capital of 1,500,000 Ffr and 250,000 Ffr for a private SCA. The same conditions apply to the financing of SCAs as apply to SAs except that SCAs can elect to include the right to variable share capital as part of their articles of association.

The supervisory board of an SCA, which has a minimum of three members none of whom can be a *commandité*, has a titular rather than an operational role, acting alongside the auditors in making recommendations to an annual general meeting of shareholders. Members of the supervisory board are appointed for a fixed term by the shareholders' meeting and can be removed from office by such a meeting. One or more *gérants* is responsible for the operational management of an SCA. This separateness of business finance and independent business management has rendered the SCA structure very attractive over recent years for management 'buy-out' initiatives. It is particularly used in cases where the former family shareholders have sold a majority interest in their company but want to continue to manage it. Yves Saint-Laurent, Michelin, Casino, WORMS are all companies with this form.

The Groupement d'Intérêt Economique (GIE)

The rise in strategic alliances in France over recent years has favoured the use of a structure called a **Groupement d'Intérêt Economique**. Companies wishing to develop their portfolios of civil or commercial facilities in common have created GIEs whose role has to be an extension of, but ancillary to, the core activity of the companies involved.

No share capital is needed to create a GIE and any directors appointed are jointly and severally accountable for respecting the legislation relating to GIEs. The articles of association for the form of undertaking can be defined in an extremely flexible way and GIEs also benefit from 'transparency' in terms of corporate taxation. On the negative side, however, participating companies are liable for any debts arising from the GIE and would also be liable for bankruptcy proceedings should the GIE be declared bankrupt. Nevertheless, the opportunity for companies to align their resources and reschedule/reassess their market penetration through such a flexible structure as a GIE means that its use is likely to grow in the coming years.

The Société en Participation

The most private of all company structures is called the 'Société en Participation'and is one in which one partner is 'invisible' to external parties whereas the visible partner is able to commit the company in all the usual commercial senses. The 'invisible' partner does not, however escape liability for any debts derived from his/her partner's activity. This form of company has no legal status and enjoys almost complete flexibility in organizing its operations as well as how it presents itself to the outside world.

Corporate taxation

We have already noted how EURL companies (an SARL with a single individual shareholder) are not liable to pay corporation tax. The same 'transparency' applies to SNCs and GIEs as well as to the *commandités* in SNC companies (*commanditaires* declare any income received as corporation tax-liable).

The usual principle of 'territoriality' means that any company earning profits in France or whose profits are the subject of a specific taxation treaty with the French authorities are liable to French tax. Corporation tax can be paid in four instalments during the financial year which runs from 1 January to 31 December.

In addition to corporation tax, any legally recognized company is required to pay an annual company tax, which varies according to the turnover of the company and ranges on a scale from 5,000 Ffr to 100,000 Ffr.

Loss-making companies in France receive favourable treatment from the tax authorities in as much as losses can be carried forward over a five-year period and set against the revenues of a specified year during that period. Deferred depreciation on fixed assets is also allowed to assist struggling companies.

Any capital which accrues from the sale of assets which have been held for less than two years are taxed at the usual corporation tax rate. Apart from gains on securities any longer term capital gains are currently taxed at the rate of 18 per cent.

Aspects of finance and the law

1   Usurious interest
The **Law of 28 December 1966** stipulates that the rate of interest on a loan must be below a maximum rate considered to be 'usurious' (**usuaire**) which is occasionally published by the Conseil National du Crédit. Criminal penalties are imposed for violation of this law which perhaps explains why there are no real credit cards in France.

2   Taux effectif global
The **TEG** (effective overall rate) must be stated in the loan agreement.

3   Consumer credit protection
The **Loi Scrivener** of 1978 obliges lenders to make a written offer of a loan with a seven-day 'cooling-off' period. The offer must include the amount of credit, the loan conditions, insurance and the TEG.

4   Bills of exchange
Lettres de change, effets de commerce or **traites** are common forms of payment in France and are frequently discounted by the banks.

5 Cheques

It is still considered a serious offence in France to issue a cheque without sufficient funds to cover it. The bank may refuse to pay a cheque for more than 100 Ffr and failure to regularize the situation within 30 days may mean withdrawal of cheque facilities and notification to the Bank of France.

6 The Loi Dailly

Under this law of 1981, a loan may be made by a bank to a corporate client, secured by transfer of the client's trade debts.

7 Litigation

In disputes between consumers and a company, cases are generally brought to the **Tribunal de Grande Instance**, whereas the **Tribunal de Commerce** deals with disputes between companies. The Tribunal de Grande Instance is made up of professional judges, whereas the Tribunal de Commerce is staffed by elected members or representatives (called **juges**) of the the local Chamber of Commerce. The Tribunal de Grande Instance's judges, however, (called **magistrats**), although they have had legal training at a Grande Ecole – the Ecole de la Magistrature – immediately become judges on qualifying rather than being lawyers who then become judges. They are often young, therefore, with no experience of practising as a lawyer. Since each local area has its own Tribunal de Grande Instance and Tribunal de Commerce, there are some 175 of the former and 230 of the latter which also have competence to deal with any commercial matter, whatever the value. If an action is brought in France, therefore, it will normally have to be where the offending party operates, however remote that may be. Variability of expertise can thus be expected and in the case of a Tribunal de Commerce, the tendency towards local bias is exacerbated by the fact that the defendant may be well known by the *juges*, fellow members of the Chamber of Commerce. There is no rule of precedent in France where the law is codified and the judges, unlike their counterparts in the UK who make the law, have the power to interpret the code with considerable latitude. Appeals can be taken to one of the thirty-five **Cours d'Appel** which, again because there is no system of precedent, tend to make their own often contradictory jurisprudence.

The legal profession

A law passed in December 1990 amalgamated the **avocats** and the **conseils juridiques**. Previously the *avocats* provided advice in all areas of law and had a monopoly of pleading before the courts. Anyone could become a *conseil juridique* (legal adviser), however, who enjoyed no monopoly and did not necessarily have to belong to one of the liberal professions (*avocat* or *notaire*). Hence banks, insurance companies, chambers of commerce and employer organizations would offer such a service. The merger of the two now establishes a monopoly of legal advice and a new profession similar to that in the USA. The *notaires* still draw up **actes authentiques** (authentic documents) necessary for all transfers of property, wills and marriages.

Employment law

Employment law sources are similar in France and in the UK and are derived from legislation, regulations, common law, collective agreements and custom and practice. However, the Codes of Practice, which are an important guide to the operation of UK employment law, do not exist in France. French employment laws and regulations have been consolidated into the **Code du travail**. This is not the case in the UK, where employment law consists of a variety of Acts and Codes of Practice. French collective agreements may receive the approval (**arrêté d'extension**) of the labour ministry. A collective sectorial agreement which has received this approval is legally binding on all employers of the relevant sector, even for the employer who is not – or is no longer – a member of the association of employers which signed the agreement. In other words, it would be of no use for an employer who does not agree with some of the terms of a convention signed by his employers' organization to leave this organization: if he did, the convention would still be legally binding on him. In practice most of the sectorial collective agreements have received ministerial approval. However, collective sectorial agreements of both countries tend to establish minima which are exceeded by most employers, especially concerning wages.

Generally speaking, while there are similarities in some areas, French and English employment laws are different in some important aspects.

- French employment law is essentially prescriptive, while UK employment law tends to be 'enabling' and therefore more open to interpretation.
- Breaches of most French Labour Code arrangements governing the relation between employers and employee representatives (**comités d'entreprise** – information and consultation, collective bargaining) are punishable by law: employers who fail to comply with them may be brought to court and subject to conviction (fines, recording of the offence on police records, notice of the offence on the plant premises and publication in newspapers).
- French employment law is more concerned with collective rights and employee representation, and goes beyond the UK law in that sphere:

for example in the UK there is no obligation on an employer to recognize a trade union whereas in France there is such an obligation and moreover French law has a number of specific requirements (number of representatives, number of paid hours off etc.). In contrast, UK employment law is more concerned with the individual employee and with the protection of his personal liberties, especially concerning trade unions.

- The legislation and practice of employment contracts are similar in both countries.
- There is no legal provision specifying recruitment and selection procedures in either country; the only regulation concerning this area are provisions which seek to prevent discrimination on the grounds of ethnic origin and sex. However, one must note that there is no legal protection against discrimination on the grounds of age in the UK, whereas that protection exists in France.
- Annual pay negotiations exist in both countries. However, in France there is a legal obligation on employers to negotiate each year on wages and in the UK collective bargaining is not determined centrally but is carried out at unit level.
- In France, manual workers' wage increases are merit-related, whereas such a practice is exceptional in the UK.
- In both countries employers intending to dismiss an employee must follow a correct procedure established for the protection of employees; the reasons that can be used by employers for fair dismissal are similar. However, two differences exist between the two systems:

  1 In the UK, correct employment procedures provide for the right of appeal against dismissal, using internal company procedures. In France there is no such legal obligation.
  2 In the UK employees must have two years' continuous service to be heard by an Industrial Tribunal (except in cases of discrimination) whereas any French employee can have recourse to the **conseil de prud'hommes** whatever his period of employment in the company.

- In France, as in the UK, the employer must consult with employees' representatives when considering a redundancy, the period of time for this being approximately the same in both countries. There are differences, however:

  1 In France the employer consults with the **comité d'entreprise** (**comité central d'entreprise et comité d'établissement**), whereas in the UK shop stewards are consulted.
  2 The procedure is more complex in France than in the UK. For individual redundancies, consultation of the *comité d'entreprise* is

not obligatory. The employee is interviewed before being notified of the redundancy. An external training programme (**convention de reconversion**) must be offered and if the employee accepts then the redundancy is immediate. If refused, the employer must notify the employee of the redundancy within seven days by registered post and also notify the local Labour Inspector.

3   In the case of more than one redundancy, the law distinguishes between below and above ten but basically the procedure is the same, very formal and strictly regulated. The employer must first consult the *délégué du personnel* and the *comités d'entreprise* who hold two meetings over a maximum two week period, often with the help of a chartered accountant appointed by the *comité d'entreprise*. The company's situation and economic reasons for the redundancies must be made thoroughly clear. The **plan social** which has been obligatory since 1989 lays out measures taken to avoid or limit redundancies and retraining packages and includes voluntary redundancy schemes. The Labour Inspector is simultaneously notified of the intention to make employees redundant. The order of redundancies is fixed by the employer based on criteria specified in the **convention collective** or workers' seniority or preferences expressed by the **comités d'entreprise**. The Labour Inspector finally has three weeks to give an opinion and suggest amendments. Letters of dismissal cannot be sent out for 30 days after notification to the Labour Inspector.

- In the UK the retirement age is 65 years for men, women being able to choose to retire at 60; in France the retirement age is 60 for both men and women.
- In France, as in the UK, there are specific tribunals for labour disputes which consist of two 'lay judges', one a representative of the employees and the other of the employer. However:

1   In France there are no tribunals of appeal; at this level, the common law tribunals, which comprise only professional judges, are competent. In the UK, tribunals exist at the appeal level (Employment Appeals Tribunal).
2   The rules governing the jurisdiction of UK and French tribunals are not the same.
3   In France the *conseil de prud'hommes* is divided into five divisions, each covering a sector of the economy, which is not the case in the UK.
4   In France, there is no institution similar to ACAS or the Central Arbitration Committee. In France there is practically no conciliation or arbitration procedure: the only ones which exist are those provided in the case of a strike which are a posteriori procedures,

and are rarely used in practice. Nor is there a Commission for Racial Equality, Equal Opportunities Commission or Wages Councils.

The **Ministère du Travail** with its district employment divisions and employment inspectors plays a very important role in France. This role mainly consists of ensuring that companies comply with labour laws and regulations; but the Ministry has also, in some cases, an advisory function (towards employers, unions and employees) and a conciliatory one in individual or collective disputes.

Union recognition within companies

British employers have much more freedom than French employers in this sphere.

In the UK, there is no legal obligation on employers to recognize one or more trade union. A union which wants to be recognized within a plant must ask the employer, and the employer may accept this demand. The acceptance of the employer depends upon several factors, the main one being the union membership among the group of employees it wants to represent: generally at least 50 per cent of the employees of a group must be members of a union in order that this union may be recognized as representing the group. The number of representatives of each union is settled by agreement between the employer and the relevant union.

In France, the five big unions (**représentés au niveau national**) are legal representatives of the employees. That means that, when a plant union belonging to one of these five big unions is instated in a plant, and provided this plant has a few members (two members are theoretically sufficient for a union to be represented), the employer cannot refuse to recognise it. The number of union representatives is specified by law according to the number of employees in the plant.

In France, as in the UK, there are two types of union representatives, the **délégués syndicaux**, who are company employees, and the **permanents syndicaux**, who are union employees at a local, regional or national level. But in France, only the *délégués syndicaux* have a role within the company; the *permanents syndicaux* at a local or national level do not intervene in the relationship between the employer and the company unions, whereas they do in the UK.

The facilities granted to the unions' representatives to enable them to carry out their duties and activities are of the same nature in France as in the UK: time off with pay, access to employees, noticeboard, use of premises, etc. There are differences, however.

- French law does not only say that these facilities exist, but specifies their exact extent, giving for instance the exact number of hours off with pay which the union representatives must have every month. UK law leaves the points to the employer's discretion or to a collective bargaining agreement.
- French unions enjoy more freedom in terms of communication with employees.

Union representatives in France are afforded far greater protection than in the UK. (There is, for example, an obligation on a French employer wishing to dismiss a union representative to seek an authorization from the Ministry.)

Rights of other employee representatives

In the UK, the employer is not legally bound to give information to joint committees or to ask them for their advice. If he chooses to do it, the extent of the information given as well as the manner in which these committees function (dates of meetings for instance) are at his discretion.

In France, the **Code du Travail** specifies the cases in which the *comité d'entreprise* must be informed and consulted, and settles in each of these cases the exact nature of the information which must be given to it. The issues on which the *comité d'entreprise* must be informed and consulted are numerous: working conditions, training plants, introduction of new technology, investment plans, sources of funding, profitability, present and future business etc.

Moreover, French law provides for the election of representatives to the Board of Directors of the firm by the *comités d'entreprise*. Even if they have only a consultative voice, they must be invited to every Board of Directors meeting. In the UK, there is no obligation of that kind on the employer.

In France, the law specifies the facilities the *comités d'entreprise* members must be given by the employer in the same way as it does for the union representatives. The *comités d'entreprise* must be given a subsidy by the employer to enable them to carry out their duties and they can ask for the services of a chartered accountant paid by the employer.

Comités d'entreprise members are afforded the same protection against dismissal as union representatives.

Industrial disputes

French and UK regulations on strikes are very different: the difference comes from the fact that there are very detailed regulations on strikes in the UK, whereas strike action is the issue over which French law gives the least detail, regulations on this topic being settled by common law, which is continually changing.

The only similarity in French and UK law over strikes is that both countries make a difference between legal and illegal strike action and attach similar consequences to that difference. In both countries unions are given a form of immunity for lawful strikes which is invalid when the strikes are unlawful: consequently the employer cannot sue unions for damages caused by a legal strike, while he may do so when the strike is illegal.

The definition of legal strikes is much narrower in the UK than in France. In the UK strike action may legally begin provided that a preliminary procedure has been adhered to. Unions may begin a strike:

- after the relevant preliminary procedures have been carried out; and
- after having organized a vote among the employees likely to be called upon to strike and after a majority of these employees have voted in favour of the strike.

When this procedure has not been followed, the strike is considered as unlawful.

In France, however:

- There is no obligatory procedure before strike action, at least in the private sector.
- There is no preliminary conciliation procedure which must be carried out before strike action.

Contrary to what happens in the UK, provided only that claims have been presented to the employer and rejected, the following strikes are legal.

- Strikes begun and carried out by the employees only, without any intervention by the unions.
- Sudden strikes: there is no obligation on employees who intend to hold a strike to forewarn of strike action.
- Strikes made by a minority of employees: providing two or more are on strike their strike action is legal.

The consequences of a strike on the employment contract of employees are not the same in the UK and in France.

- In the UK an employee who strikes may be dismissed.
- In France it is a principle that an employee may not be dismissed for

striking, except when he has committed extremely serious misconduct (French concept of **faute lourde**).

Finally, contrary to what happens in the UK, French Tribunals consider that an employer who institutes a lock-out, except in very specific cases, does not show respect for the terms of the contracts of employment. Therefore, French employers practically never institute lock-outs.

Health and safety

There are no great differences between the UK and French legislation: every failure to respect health and safety regulations is punishable by law, the responsibility for the offence belonging to the plant managers.

Employee communication

In France as in the UK there are few legal obligations on employers concerning employee communication. In French law, there is no other obligation on the employer than to place the **bilan social** (showing employment statistics and salaries) at the employees' disposal, whereas the only obligation in UK law is that the employer traditionally includes a paragraph on employee communications in the annual report to shareholders.

Conclusion

We noted at the beginning of this chapter that no detailed legal definition exists for the term **fonds de commerce**. There also exist multiple forms of companies whose structure and operation are substantially less regulated than one might expect in a country known for the traditional influence of the state over business activity and strategic planning. The constraints surrounding the *Sociétés de Capitaux* are balanced by the flexibility of the *Sociétés de Personnes*. This apparent tension between the regulated and the deregulated mirrors the challenge facing French legislators over the coming years. The legislators have loosened many of the legal ties which held French business back from playing its full role in the international arena and effectively prevented substantial foreign investment in France. However, they have still much to do to apply employment legislation, and in spite of decrees in 1990 and 1992, foreign investors from outside the European Union still encounter difficulties in practice when wishing to invest in existing businesses in France.

4 Business and finance

Introduction

Two notable changes occurred in the French financial scene in the 1980s: a gradual but fundamental reform of the banking sector and a general shift away from reliance on debt towards equity as a source of external finance. These two changes have been underscored by a whole paraphernalia of new financial instruments and engineering methods which are leading to radically changing views on ownership, management and structures of companies.

Banking

The period of greatest expansion in the banking sector occurred between 1967 and 1975, following the reform of 1966 which allowed banks more flexibility to set interest rates and to open new branches, with the aim of shifting the burden of providing investment funds from the state to the banking sector. Until the 1960s some 80 per cent of investment financing emanated from state sources. During the late 1960s and 1970s the financing of investment by banks increased from 38 per cent (1965) to 60 per cent (1974), while the capital markets played a very minor role. The banks were essentially the main financial intermediaries.

The concentration of industry was mirrored by a similar process in the banking sector, as many local banks disappeared (245 in 1945 and 63 in 1975), together with a number of merchant banks (43 in 1946, 17 in 1975). The period was dominated by the deposit banks **Banque Nationale de Paris**, **Crédit Lyonnais**, **Société Générale** (all nationalized) and the two merchant banks **Paribas** and **Indosuez**, but the mutualist and cooperative banks also expanded rapidly to compete both on interest rates and number of branches.

By the 1980s, there was a growing crisis in the financial system:

- The increasing number of clients using cheques (for which there is still no charge in France) was rapidly increasing overheads.
- There was growing unemployment in banks as those hired in the 1960s and 1970s were laid off to make way for new technology.
- There were some sixty-five privileged loan schemes, sixty-eight different types of subsidy being offered by different privileged compartments of the system (e.g. **Crédit Agricole** which had a monopoly of preferential loans to agriculture), which led to 48 per cent of credit to the economy being allocated through specialized and diverse lending establishments. All had so many different statutes, rights and privileges that competition became hopelessly distorted with a resulting high cost of credit. Because of such distortions the task of the Banque de France regulating the economy by interest rates was infinitely more difficult than that of its much more independent German counterpart, the Bundesbank. Until joining the ERM, France's attempts at controlling inflation had hence been much less successful (see Table 4.1).
- The growing importance of the capital market, particularly after the tax incentives of 1979, started a gradual tendency for savings to move from shorter to longer types of investments (unit trusts – **SICAV** – became particularly attractive and still represent one of the most vigorous markets in Europe).
- The low equity base of French banks was of continuing concern.

This crisis was characterized by a gradual process of disintermediation, i.e. less indirect and more direct financing via the capital markets, which large companies were finding more profitable. French firms increasingly switched to building up equity and reducing debt, with the result that the proportion of new equity issues rose from 8.4 per cent of new external resources in 1982 to 25.5 per cent in 1987, although in 1988 and 1989 there was a sharp upturn in short-term credit after the October crash in 1987.

All this meant less custom for the banks at a time of growing costs (labour in the early 1980s representing two-thirds of overheads) and led to an overall drop in profitability.

Most of the banking sector was nationalized in 1982, a process which involved thirty-six banks (thirty-four deposit and two merchant banks) and provided the state with control of over 80 per cent of both loans and credits. Reasons for such nationalization were partly classical Socialist ideology, but there was a genuine concern to introduce a more efficient system of monetary control, by decompartmentalizing the system and allowing all of the various types of establishment to offer the same services in terms of loans and deposits. This process had already started under the previous government in 1979 with the introduction of the savings accounts and the **Livret d'Epargne Populaire** (LEP) and the **Compte de Dévéloppement Industriel** (CODEVI) which all banks were

Table 4.1 *French inflation (1982–1992)*

Year	(%)
1982	9.7
1983	9.3
1984	6.7
1985	4.7
1986	2.1
1987	3.4
1988	3.5
1989	3.5
1990	3.4
1991	3.2
1992	2.5
1993	2.1
1994	1.7
1995	2.0 (Forecast)

Source: OECD

entitled to offer. Two Acts, one in 1982 and a second in 1984, made all establishments covered by the same law, excluding the Treasury, the Banque de France and the powerful Caisse des Dépôts. In reality, the many different networks have not disappeared, but they can all offer the same products. There are still four big categories.

- The high street and merchant banks.
- The mutualist and cooperative sector.
- The **Sociétés Financières**, specializing in leasing, hire purchase, etc.
- The specialist state-controlled financial institutions, e.g. Crédit Foncier, Crédit National, which are still the main distributors of state credit for industrial investments and whose loans are often subject to the National Plan.

The right-wing Chirac government of 1986 planned to sell off Société Générale, Crédit Lyonnais, BNP, Paribas, Indosuez and Crédit Agricole. Only three reverted to the private sector, however: Société Générale (SocGen), Paribas and Indosuez. Essentially these six banks, together with the insurance companies and the **Caisse des Dépôts**, make up the major institutional investors (see p. 62) and the partial success of the privatization programme under Chirac posed the fundamental questions of how effective the programme could possibly be when some of the major shareholders of these same privatized companies were still in state hands and thus subject to a degree of subtle, although officially denied, manipulation. To this issue was added another, that of the *noyau dur*, the hard core of faithful investors approached by the Chirac government to acquire stakes in the newly privatized companies. The in-coming Socialist government of 1988 accused the Chirac government of approaching those companies which gave financial support to the right-wing parties, and there was some debate over ways of dismantling the *noyau dur* before the legal time limit imposed on the shareholders to retain the shares. Certainly the ensuing saga points to the very thin line which exists between the influence of political and financial clans and the workings of the market place in France. It was to prevent a repeat performance that under the privatization programme of the previous Balladur government the privatization commission was set up, comprising six 'independent' members whose task it is to recommend suitable companies for the *noyau dur*. In theory, however, the government has the right to reject its recommendations.

As recession brought the collapse of the property market and a large crop of bankruptcies, 1992 was a catastrophic year for the banks. The global drop in profits was 30 per cent as banks were caught between a sharp increase in risk, thereby obliging them to set aside an additional 30 per cent in provisions and a steep rise in operating costs. Some of the risks were highly publicized, such as the collapse of the Maxwell empire, but the main problem was the number of small firms going bankrupt. The ambitious expansion programmes of Suez and Crédit Lyonnais, particularly the latter's sorry and costly venture into the Hollywood film industry, were heavily penalized. Altogether, the three **vieilles dames** (the ex-state owned Société Générale and BNP and the still nationalized Crédit Lyonnais) only managed a third of their 1991 earnings. Crédit Agricole, however, managed to buck the trend by an increase of 6 per cent. Paribas emerged with a small profit but Suez plunged back into the red, thus posing the question of whether they are big enough to remain real merchant and investment banks.

Crédit Lyonnais, Crédit Agricole and BNP are still three of the world's largest banks (Crédit Lyonnais alone is by balance sheet the biggest non-Japanese bank and has the largest European network of 900 branches outside France), but with the present major confrontation between the big three deposit banks, Crédit Agricole and the savings banks (**caisses d'épargne**), profitability is in serious doubt in the mass banking sector, particularly with the Post Office (**La Poste**) network entering the fray and competing for private customers' accounts. There is even the belief that in this congested, overbanked situation, one of the major banks might well disappear. At the medium-size level, banks such as the Crédit Mutuel, CIC and the Banques Populaires aim either to gain sufficient market share in the regions to stay in the mass market or to exploit profitable niches. But recession has only heightened the intense competition which was fundamentally caused by the deregulation of the 1980s, during a period when operating costs have been at their highest. In addition, a phenomenon particular to France, **les SICAV monétaires** (money funds), offering far higher returns than the traditional savings accounts, have drained the banks' resources and obliged them to 'buy' from the money market at higher prices. Interest margins – the mainstay of French banking profits – fell from 5 per cent in 1987 to 3.4 per cent in 1992, which has coincided with an overall drop in demand for borrowing. Indeed, the situation was such in early 1993 that Standard and Poors placed eight of the top banks **sous surveillance** (under surveillance) because of the increase in their burden of risk and running costs. Such a move incurred the wrath of the Governor of the Banque de France, who believed that too much weight was being given to property investments and that the banks were, in effect, adequately supervised as **établissements de crédit**.

Recovery is now well under way, however, as recession has receded, productivity increases after the major effort made in this direction and the level of provisions declines. Nevertheless, the banks are faced with major changes in their environment. First, the Banque de France has changed its status, becoming virtually free of the government for decisions on monetary policy. According to Article 1 of its revised constitution *'La Banque de France définit et met en oeuvre la politique monétaire dans le but d'assurer la stabilité des prix'* (the Bank of France defines and implements monetary policy with the aim of ensuring price stability). Moreover, *'dans l'exercice de ces attributions le gouverneur ne peut ni solliciter ni accepter des instructions du gouvernement ou de toute autre personne'* (in exercising these powers, the governor may neither seek nor accept instructions from the government or any other person). Exchange rates are still fixed by the government however, under Article 2, and hence the true nature of the Banque de France's independence is belied since ultimately exchange rates and monetary policy are intimately linked.

The second major change in the banking environment will be the reform of the Caisse des Dépôts, which will be considered below under a separate heading since, as the single most powerful institutional investor, it merits particular attention. Thirdly, the privatization of both banks and insurance companies, more than any other factor, will radically change the French financial landscape as the state, in principle, no longer exercises the same control. Hitherto, the state appointed the heads of both state-owned banks and insurance companies, and the government's choice was invariably a civil servant who in turn recruited others from the same ministries. This occurred with companies in the non-finance sector, too (even private companies end up with ex-civil servants in charge), and is at the heart of the criticism that, over time, some large companies have been less than efficient, principally because such a system produces a bureaucratic mentality and a reluctance to shed labour. On interest rates, too, although the government insisted on the fact that the two nationalized banks behaved in exactly the same way as their private counterparts.

During the recent bouts of speculation against the franc, the Banque de France raised its short-term interest rates but the government insisted on the banks holding their rates, thereby causing them to incur big losses. State banks were always the first to drop and the last to increase their rates. In theory, the shareholders of the newly privatized banks and insurance companies will be able to appoint professional financiers as heads but in practice, the present culture may still prevail, as was shown to be the case with the appointment at the private SocGen of a civil servant as head. Prior to privatization too (BNP was privatized in 1993), heads were changed in several companies to reflect government preferences by appointing trusted, well-connected members of the Balladur coterie. All were civil servants and had been heads of other state companies. Privatization, therefore, may well be the opportunity for financial institutions to behave as freely as their overseas counterparts but the reality of the French business culture may well dictate otherwise. Such new-found freedom may be more efficient but whether it will be more effective is still open to doubt. The behaviour of the new *noyau dur* members may be crucial since they include non-French companies (BAT, Kuwaiti Oil in the case of BNP) who will have no truck with low profits. They may well represent the best guarantee against future meddling by the government. The most decisive factor, however, will be the privatization in turn of the state-owned companies who represent in some cases the largest shareholders.

Final factors in the challenges still pressurizing the banks are ageing workforces and overmanning, in spite of vigorous programmes of labour shedding and unprofitable international networks. The banks still have much to do both to restore profitability and to cope with profound changes in their environment. Strategic choices will be crucial as Crédit Lyonnais retrenches from its lone all-out expansion both at home and overseas, SocGen continues with its preference for niche markets and BNP's confused attempts, in an alliance with the Dresdner Bank, to play both ends in its desire both to be the bank of all France – it already has the largest retail operation in France but is clashing head-on with Crédit Agricole, La Poste, the *caisses d'epargne* and the other deposit banks – and to break into the financial engineering and asset management markets.

Since they have both played distinct and crucial roles, two unique institutions are worth closer study: Crédit Agricole and the Caisse des Dépôts.

Crédit Agricole

In contrast to the problems of other French banks, the Crédit Agricole has known striking financial success even through the recent recession. Founded in 1894, as a mutual *caisse*, it is the most profitable of French banks and the richest in Europe in terms of equity. In spite of its 8,380 branches and managing 1,000 bn Ffr through 15.5 million accounts, it enjoys better levels of productivity than the other big three (SocGen, BNP, Crédit Lyonnais). Amongst its customers are included not only farmers and rural households, but also urban households, professional people, local authorities, PME and large companies. It has an important international network in spite of difficulties experienced at the end of the 1980s and owns Prédica, the second biggest life insurance company in France, where **bancassurance** has firmly taken hold. Its original and peculiar structure of regional and local organizations (*caisses* being governed by private law and the state controlling the national federation *caisse nationale*) was changed in 1988, when the local and regional branches bought out the central *caisse*, in what was, in effect, a privatization operation under the Socialists. Immediately after the Second World War, however, it had no branches at all, its activities essentially being conducted by the mayor's assistant or a retired employee. Its expansion came in the 1960s, with the opening of local branches and its rapidity was due to one of its key characteristics and advantages, that of being close to its customers. In 1959, it was authorized to offer mortgages and in 1967 to distribute the same products as other banks. In 1979 it lost the tax advantages so despised by the other banks, when it was permitted to offer its services to non-members.

Its original purpose was to help provide funds to farmers and peasants crippled by interest of often over 100 per cent charged by local usurers. The capital of those members wishing to save was put at the disposal of those needing to borrow. Such was the peasants' mistrust of borrowing, however, and the low level of savings, that the state intervened by forcing the Banque de France, then still private, to pay the Crédit Agricole an advance of 40 bn Ffr followed by an annual sum if it wanted to keep its monopoly of issuing money. This, then, was the start of the subsidized loans (*prêts bonifiés*) which helped to transform the face of French farming, particularly after the Second World War, as the *caisses* distributed long-term loans to small farmers, cooperatives and agricultural mutual societies. In 1920, 60 per cent of its funds were still of state origin. Early diversification came in the 1920s as the *caisses* were opened to artisans and local authorities for electrification purposes. At the end of the 1930s there was an abundance of money in the countryside with few opportunities to invest, a situation which led to hoarding. One of the Crédit Agricole's most enduring savings instruments, to tap this cash, was five-year bonds.

The agricultural sector in France is still the largest in Europe in spite of falling incomes, the rapid drop in the number of farmers, the set-aside policy and the prospect of more and more countryside becoming deserted. The farming community is slowly coming round to the reality of less protection and that it will have to win foreign markets with fewer subsidies. Meanwhile, Crédit Agricole increased its profit of 4.5 bn Ffr in 1989 to 5.3 bn Ffr in 1993 and so attracted criticism that it is betraying the agriculture sector and food industry by moving in other strategic directions. Obsession with banking, finance and globalization has led to abandonment of farmers and peasants. The reality is, however, that it still accounts for 80 per cent of all credit given to farmers and, in spite of the phasing out of the *prêts bonifiés* by the state, it still managed 92.6 per cent of these loans in 1992 (BNP can now also distribute them). But with agricultural investment falling, Crédit Agricole is obliged to diversify, even to the extent of advising the government on the privatization of Renault and structuring the financing of new tram networks in such towns as Caen.

There is no doubt that the vegetable growers, pig farmers and dairy cooperatives of Britanny could not have been possible without the Crédit Agricole. It is a major employer in its own right, with its multitude of branches, and provides rural employment through aid to artisans and peasant farmers. So the major question now is, will it continue to help transform French agriculture and exports, fund regional development and aid both big and small farmers? The fear is that it will become a bank like all the others and lose its identity.

Caisse des Dépôts

Traditionally a bank, but now the major institutional investor on the Bourse where it makes its biggest profit (4.3 bn Ffr in 1993), the Caisse des Dépôts is not subject to the banking laws, even though it is officially an *établissement de crédit*. In a modern, liberal economy it attracts much criticism and even more jealousy for having a totally anachronistic structure with a head appointed by the president. The main bone of contention is its war-chest of some 45 bn Ffr in shares, property and holding companies, principally financed through its monopoly of the social security system's cash, funds received by *notaires*, the Livret 'A' account of its national network of *caisses d'epargne* with which it finances council dwellings (**HLM – habitations à loyer modéré**) and its management of more than 400 bn Ffr of retirement and savings funds, e.g. for local authority workers. It is a financial, industrial and services group with many overlapping departments and activities, some in the public sector, and many highly competitive with the private sector, such as the property market, local development, transport networks, cable television and even car-park and ski-lift management.

There is no doubt that it is in need of serious reform to bring clarity and order to its structure, but whatever the extent of the changes, it will remain a powerful tool for the state in its financing of the economy. Privatization was once mooted but the government rejected the idea of giving up such a convenient institution to regulate markets through its enormous financial power and presence, too, on the Bourse. In its time it has been a cash-cow for the state, providing money to recapitalize Crédit Lyonnais (1.5 bn Ffr) to refloat the Crédit d'Équipement des PME, to salvage Air France (1.5 bn Ffr) and to tide over the periodic deficits of the social security system (in 1993, it provided 120 bn Ffr to keep the system afloat for 2–3 days). With fewer **zinzins** (institutional investors) left after privatization, the government feels it needs to maintain a major influence on the stock markets, even though its use by the Left in the raid on the Société Générale at the end of the 1980s drew much criticism from parties on the Right.

Reform has been focused on a three-tier structure separating its various activities but it is generally viewed as somewhat cosmetic and superficial. One other major reason for the government's unwillingness to go further were the social implications, as with the situation at Air France and the privatization of Renault, where the state decided to keep a 51 per cent stake. Since the announcement of the reform at the Caisse des Dépôts, some 5,000–6,000 workers have rejoined the trade unions and a strike called by the CGT and CFDT attracted a 40 per cent following. The fundamental problem with this and other state-owned companies is the status of the workforce, which is difficult to reconcile with the competitive activities of a company governed by private law. One solution adopted at France Télécom was for employees to be placed on 'detachment' for any activity other than public service.

At La Poste, too, similar fears are being expressed as postal workers are anxious over both job losses and privatization, in a context of huge losses incurred over the mounting use of faxes and the prospect of the introduction of a smart-card for the payment of the **feuille d'assurance-maladie** (health system document completed for all visits to doctors, hospitals and chemists), at present sent through the post.

The insurance sector

Insurance companies have not been spared the worst of the recession, particularly through the property slump, difficulties with their banking arms and problems over recovery in the damage insurance sector. But one fear has not materialized and that is of penetration by large multinationals into the French market. Hitherto, all attempts have failed and in the large risk market foreign companies even have a smaller market share than five years ago.

Insurance is one of France's major business sectors and is currently the fifth largest in the world. There are some 550 insurance companies and mutual benefit organizations (**les mutuelles**) with offices and agents in most towns. *Les mutuelles* are organizations formed to represent a particular professional, trade or occupational sector, e.g. teachers, civil servants etc., to insure themselves at favourable premiums. Theoretically, they are non-profit-making. After all costs, any excess is paid to members, held in reserve or re-invested. In the main they provide supplementary health insurance schemes and pensions and market their services directly by telephone or mail, as opposed to the use of **agents généraux** (general agents) or **courtiers** (brokers), as used by most other insurance companies.

One major development has been the challenge mounted by the banks to the insurance companies. In 1983, 60 per cent of life insurance policies were sold by UAP, GAN and AGF, the main state-owned companies (UAP is now privatized). In 1994, banks accounted for 60 per cent of life policies. UAP, once the leading insurance company, was relegated to third in 1993, with a turnover of 22 bn Ffr. Prédica, the insurance arm of Crédit Agricole – and there are many cross shareholdings between banks and insurance companies – had a turnover of 30 bn Ffr. Two main reasons explain the success of the banks' incursion. First, the contracts issued by the banks are clear, simple and very flexible, allowing withdrawal with minimum penalties and with no front-loading of administration charges. Secondly, the banks have large distribution networks with fewer overheads than the traditional insurers whose agents and brokers are expensive. With banks, insurance products can be sold during other transactions, whereas insurance companies have to go out and seek their customers and pay commission. Hence, a 10,000 franc investment costs 190 Ffr to transact with Crédit Lyonnais, but 2,400 Ffr with GAN. Insurance companies also have difficulty in responding to competition by proposing new, cheaper products because their agents react and refuse to contemplate any reduction in commission. In such circumstances, AGF were only able to increase turnover by 7 per cent in 1993, but Prédica by 75 per cent. Hypermarkets, too, pose a significant and growing threat, with Carrefour now offering its own life insurance policies. The general response of the traditional insurers is to concentrate on damage insurance as their major priority. They are also banking on changes in the generous social security scheme to generate the pension and health insurance side. Overall, insurance represented 3 per cent of household expenditure in 1975 and 5 per cent in 1991. Most of this figure is accounted for by car insurance but the major increase has been in life insurance, especially policies coupled with savings and retirement schemes, no tax being payable if retained for more than eight years. The largest life insurer is the **Comptoir National de Prévoyance**, once part of Caisses des Dépôts but now independent and selling its policies through both the Ecureuil and the post office *caisse d'épargne* networks.

Savings and investment

Until well into 1993, the main form of savings in France were the money funds already mentioned (*SICAV monétaires*) which guaranteed a tax-free 10 per cent return. These funds were essentially invested in *Certificats de Dépôts* (Certificates of Deposits – CDs) and 3–6 month treasury bonds. With the drop in interest rates, this has fallen sharply to 6 per cent, with bonds and life insurance being the main beneficiaries. As has been seen, the effect of these SICAV on banks' own resources was catastrophic and they even had to resort to issuing CDs at 10 per cent. Savers no longer invested in property, shares or the Caisse d'Epargne Livret 'A', which offered a paltry tax-free 4.5 per cent. Such funds are banned in Germany and there were loud cries for making them taxable. The government feared a flight of capital and penalizing low-income savers, but the general reaction was that the high savers were already investing in Luxembourg and the rich savers of Carpentras (the town taken as a common reference point for wealth measurement) were only likely to go to the local bank. As for low income earners, tax is not significant on savings.

Life insurance now represents half of French household savings (a relatively high level of 12.5 per cent of GDP) but there has been a noticeable return to favour of other schemes such as the **plan d'épargne-logement** (PEL) – a linked savings/mortgage scheme – and the **plan d'épargne en actions** (PEA). The PEL pay 6 per cent net of tax with 50 per cent of the working population subscribing to such a scheme. Low-interest mortgages can be obtained after a set number of years of saving. They too suffered in the early 1990s from the money funds, with savers not wanting loans (**les bons frères**) turning to the SICAV, whilst the demand for loans increased. With lower interest now payable on other forms of savings incoming funds exceeded loans. The banks wanted to see the 6 per cent net lowered (it was eventually reduced to 5.25 per cent in 1994), to enable them to lower rates on their deposit accounts (**compte sur livret** – banks are not allowed in France to pay interest on *current* accounts) but it was feared this would be too unpopular if the Livret 'A' rate of 4.5 per cent was also lowered. The government was also pushing the PEL hard to stimulate the property market.

The PEA (a share savings scheme, not unlike PEPs) has been highly successful since its launch in 1992, again mainly due to the tax exemptions allowed if money was transferred from money funds to the PEA (this was also true of the highly successful Balladur bond of 1993).

One other savings scheme is the **plan d'épargne populaire** (PEP – similar to the British 'Tessa's'), created by Bérégovoy, then Finance Minister, in 1990 with a number of tax advantages if left in the account for up to 8–10 years.

Interest rates and tax treatment are critical to the government's financial strategy of wishing to shift savings from short to long-term instruments whilst safeguarding the popular savings, providing finance for HLM and support for the PME. The Livret 'A' sums up the dilemma, since lowering its rate would harm HLM construction, if savings were diverted elsewhere, but at the same time the PME need lower rates on bank loans – only possible if banks can offer less on savings accounts. Distinctions are being blurred, too, with the *caisses d'épargne* issuing cash withdrawal cards for the Livret 'A', a move tantamount to remunerating current accounts.

Finally, in spite of the hype and promises surrounding the necessity to create pension funds in France, the government does not now seem to be in a hurry to make firm proposals. A commission set up before the 1993 national elections recommended British-style pension funds administered to companies and controlled externally by the **Commission de contrôle des assurances** (Insurance Control Commission). Industrialists preferred German-style pension funds, however, where funds form part of a company's capital as 'quasi-capital'. The government's objection is that if tax advantages were given they would drain money away from an already fragile budget.

Stock markets

Throughout the 1980s, the Bourse grew in importance as the direct result of tax changes favouring equity investment by individuals (particularly through unit trusts) and of disinflation and the consequent switch by companies to equity. The privatization issues of 1986 greatly swelled the ranks of private investors from 1.5 million in 1986 to 6.2 million in 1987. Since then, there was a steady decline until 1992 (4.5 m), since which date there has been an increase of 27 per cent (5.7 m), largely due to the privatization issues of 1993/1994. Overall, however, with the flattening out of the numbers of unit trust holders – one-quarter of the population held unit or investment trusts in 1991, but only one-fifth in 1992 – there has been a steady decline in the numbers of holders of securities. In spite of the growth of importance of the stock market, however, it is still true to say that French companies have the lowest equity base in the western World. Because of the pay-as-you-go state pension scheme (**répartition**) and the consequent lack of pension funds (**capitalisation**) there is nobody to invest to provide long-term capital and stimulate the Bourse, restore companies' profits and so enable them to form reserves, pay off debt and be more attractive to investors. In addition, many companies are family-owned and prefer their shares not to be quoted for fear of losing control. Where companies are quoted, a complex web of cross-shareholdings prevents takeover bids, thus explaining why British investment in France, although large overall, is nearly always in small companies.

France has seven stock exchanges: one in Paris (the seventh largest in the world); and six in various towns and provinces, the second most important being Lyon. Since January 1991, all quotations on the regional bourses have been integrated into a national system centred on the Paris bourse. In Paris, the old outcry method on the forward market (**à terme**), which accounts for the greatest value of trading, has been replaced by a computerized system giving continuous quotations. Prices are still fixed daily on the spot or cash market (**comptant**), which comprises a greater number of stocks, although capitalization is less than the forward market. For those companies wishing fewer strict formalities, there is the over-the-counter market (**marché hors côte**).

The big success of the 1980s was undoubtedly the equivalent of the unlisted securities market – the 'Second Marché' set up in 1983. Its popularity was largely due to the less onerous conditions imposed on companies than on the official market. Only a minimum of 10 per cent of shares have to be offered and a complete prospectus is not required. In the early days, new issues were frequently oversubscribed many times, making it the largest market in Europe. At present, however, more investors are needed on the Second Marché where companies are literally dying through lack of finance. The great rush into venture capital, although France is the third biggest market after the USA and UK, has been transformed into almost complete collapse, especially for the SDR (**Sociétés de Développement Régional**) which find themselves with unsellable minority holdings in PME. These are desperately short of finance but unattractive because of the drop in their profits and the value of their assets.

Other changes were made in the system in the 1980s. The previous stockbrokers (**agents de change**) were all appointed by the Ministry of Finance, which also fixed commissions. They alone could deal in shares on the stock exchange – there were no market-makers – and they also monopolized the market for French government bonds. The break-up of their monopoly started under the Socialists but to speed the process of reform a new market was set up in 1987 to deal with government bonds. This business transacted by twelve market-makers is now proving more lucrative than the equivalent London market shared by double the number of dealers. Since 1988, any French or overseas concern has been able to buy one of the stockbroking firms (now called **Sociétés de Bourse**) whose monopoly was set to end in 1992 (fixed commission went in 1990). Many are in dire need of such an injection of funds having lost vast sums of money on the new futures market, the **MATIF**, whose regulations have now been accordingly tightened up. Principal buyers of the stockbrokers have been the banks, which have long fretted at the commission they paid the brokers although the majority of orders come through the banks.

The performance of the Bourse (850 quoted companies) has, by and large, mirrored that of the London Stock Exchange, standing at the end of 1994 at a level 88 per cent higher than after the October crash of 1987 (London 84.3 per cent). In particular there has been an explosion of government bonds (78 per cent of the total). At the time of writing 1995 has been a poor year, however, underlining the Bourse's vulnerability to foreign investment funds.

Credit-rating agencies

Having made a comparatively recent appearance on the French financial scene, the agencies of Standard and Poors, Moody's and the European IBCA are gradually exerting considerable influence, although at the same time upsetting many. BNP had to wait several months for a rating from Standard and Poors, which prevented it from proceeding with a big bond issue. Crédit Lyonnais had a similar experience at the hands of Moody's. One particular criticism is that they are excluding some borrowers from the market, doubtless due to the fact that they are still not well known in France and hence would-be investors are unsure of what the ratings and, particularly innocuous changes in ratings, mean precisely. With the state rating triple AAA and accounting for 70.5 per cent of domestic bond issues, other financial institutions often with only slightly lower ratings find it difficult to attract investors. In the main, ratings are sought and paid for by companies, although unsolicited ratings also exist.

Taxation

There are few observers who are not agreed that the whole tax structure in France is badly in need of reform to solve the problem of growing expenditure on the health system, unemployment and pensions, at present to a large extent paid for by social security contributions (see Table 4.2). With TVA (**Taxe sur la Valeur Ajoutée** – VAT) now accounting for 45 per cent of all tax receipts, the spotlight is particularly on income tax which, with its low yield, complexity and chaotic progressiveness, is so unintelligible that it is rarely criticized as being unfair because quite simply most of the French taxpayers do not understand it.

In all, some eight operations including calculating entitlement to a number of shares or **parts** according to size of family or dependants, and a Byzantine series of both reductions and increases, are necessary before knowing how much tax is due. Amongst its major drawbacks is that it

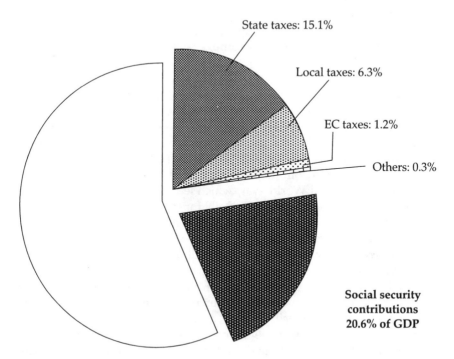

Taxes: 22.9% of GDP

State taxes: 15.1%

Local taxes: 6.3%

EC taxes: 1.2%

Others: 0.3%

**Social security
contributions
20.6% of GDP**

Figure 4.1   *Taxation in 1992. Source: Le Monde, 9.3.93*

is too concentrated on a small number of taxpayers – only 50 per cent of families pay – and is very progressive in the middle income bracket, whilst very sudden and sharp between the minimum wage (SMIC = 6,010 Ffr) and 7,000 francs. Those on very low salaries are not taxed at all but by paying social security contributions on the very first franc they earn, actually have an actual tax rate of 18 per cent. Those earning in excess of 200,000 Ffr annually – 10 per cent of the population and earning one-third of declared income – pay two-thirds of total income tax receipts but only one-third of both income tax and social security contributions. The overall need is to reconcile social security contributions, which are large, proportional and paid by all, with income tax payments which are confidential, progressive, unevenly distributed and liable to be evaded by the self-employed.

One major reform would be to deduct tax at source instead of allowing payment in three tranches (or ten monthly payments) directly by individuals to the tax authorities. Such a move, although highly desirable and likely to generate more tax (income tax accounts for 13 per cent of tax receipts, in contrast to an average 30 per cent in other industrialized countries) is likely to run into stiff resistance precisely because of its enormous inequality which favours many. In particular, the retired benefit from generous reductions to the extent that their purchasing power is now greater than that of the employed. Seventy per cent of the wealth tax (**impôt de solidarité sur la fortune**) is actually paid by those over 60.

Accounting

The French state has played a major role in the development of accounting, whereas in the UK and the USA the accounting profession has by and large been allowed to regulate itself. Much of the state's involvement in France has sprung from the need for reconstruction of the economy at the end of the Second World War, which led to a series of five-year economic plans. The essential tool originally for the economic control implied by these plans was accounting but on a nationally standardized basis which could provide useful economic data. The **Plan Comptable Général** (PCG) was devised with this in mind and although initially only applied to nationalized companies, its use was extended to the private sector. Essentially it is an all-purpose national accounting code of some 400 pages and is the responsibility of the **Conseil National de la Comptabilité**, the French national accounting council.

A second way in which the state intervened in accounting was the fact that the PCG was also made available to tax collectors to measure tax liability. As a result the whole system became tax-driven with firms seeking to minimize tax liability rather than provide essential information for shareholders. The lesser role played by the Bourse in capital allocation means that accountants are not as prominent in business as in the UK and, as French accounts are based on historical costs, they are more conservative in nature. French accounting and financial reporting are being increasingly influenced, however, by international investment and capital markets and the European Fourth Directive (which introduced the notion of notes to the accounts and the idea of 'true and fair' (**image fidèle**) in 1983). Nevertheless, in spite of these pressures towards greater convergence, the PCG seems set to remain a permanent feature of the accounting landscape in France.

The accounting and auditing professions

One distinctive feature is the existence of two separate bodies for accounting and auditing. Auditors (**commissaires aux comptes**) conduct the statutory audit and 'expert accountants' (**experts comptables**) prepare the accounts. As with other professions (doctors, pharmacists, architects), they are organized into **ordres**, which are administered by their members but ultimately controlled by the government. The auditors belong to the **Compagnie des Commissaires aux Comptes** (an *ordre* in spite of its name) and accountants to the **Ordre des Experts Comptables et des Comptables Agréés** (the latter are 'qualified accountants' whose numbers are rapidly decreasing since the abolition of the qualification in 1972). Membership, however, is practically the same for both groups. This is because firms are organized to provide both accounting services and audits but the auditor is legally prohibited from providing any other service to a client whose accounts he audits. It is thus impossible for one physical person to act as both commissaire and expert-accountant to the same business. Commissaires may not provide non-audit services and expert-accountants can offer ancillary services such as tax, legal, computing and other advice only if they also provide accounting. The leading firms are shown in Table 4.2. Confusingly, accounting and auditing firms can form agreements to provide services but are not allowed to advertise.

In 1990, there were 10,927 *expert comptables* and 1,703 qualified accountants registered with the Ordre and 9,666 commissaires with the Compagnie. The average size of firms (**cabinets**) employing accountants is ten, with a total of 6,000 cabinets of which only 1,000 have more than twenty employees. Some 95,000 accountants work in *cabinets*, whilst 3,000 are self-employed. It should be noted, however, that only 50 per cent of accountants join *cabinets* or operate as sole practitioner on qualifying. The other half immediately join industry and commerce in which case they are barred from being members of the Ordre.

The diploma necessary to become an *expert comptable* is the **diplôme d'expertise comptable** which is organized in five phases lasting at least seven years after obtaining the *baccalauréat*. Phase four is a three-year training period in an accounting firm as a full-time employee. Phases 3 and 5 lead to obligatory examination but possession of a **maîtrise des sciences et techniques comptables et financières** after four years of university study allows phases 1 and 2 to be waived. The number qualifying each year has risen to around 1,000 (1990) from under 300 in the early 1970s.

Accountants' professional training is primarily based on the PCG and therefore the mental approach adopted is more akin to that of lawyers, with its emphasis on the written law rather than the judgemental and decision-oriented training of Anglo-Saxon accountants.

Conclusion

The ways in which business in France has financed itself have undergone dramatic change since the Second World War. From a situation where

Table 4.2   *Leading firms in 1989/90*

Firm	Staff	Turnover (F.m) Total	Turnover (F.m) Accounting	Audit
KPMG Fiduciaire de France	4,496	1,897	1,376	521
Fiducial	3,484	1,040	1,040	0
HSD-Castel (Ernst & Young)	995	676	0	676
Befec (Price Waterhouse)	1,130	670	0	670
Barbier-Frinault Fiduciaire (Arthur Andersen)	875	611	0	611
ACL Audit (Coopers & Lybrand)	1,037	537	0	537
BDA (Deloitte, Ross, Tohmatsu)	910	498	0	498
Guerard Viala	520	275	0	275
SOFIDEX	805	258	258	0
Salustro Reydel	394	233	0	233
Eurex	628	204	204	0
Calan-Ramolino	400	186	0	186
Mazars	250	155	0	155

Source: Scheid J.-C. and Walton P., 1992, p. 112

the state directly provided much of the finance the emphasis was gradually switched in the 1960s and 1970s to the banks as providers. The 1980s saw another fundamental development with the growing importance of the Bourse, fuelled by the government's attempts to encourage savers to invest in more long-term forms of savings, particularly through the medium of the SICAV (unit trusts).

Nevertheless, by comparison with their counterparts in other industrialized countries French companies are under-capitalized and hence the next transformation in the financial scene is vital. Privatization is the spur but without the help of pension funds to invest the Bourse will continue to lack liquidity. The state's bloated social security system needs urgent reform, which could well give rise not only to Anglo-Saxon type pension funds but in turn to a major overhaul of the taxation system which remains unfair, illogical and insufficient. France's pay-as-you-go scheme, therefore, lies at the very heart of the new challenge facing the country: whether to face up to the necessity for reform of its sacrosanct welfare system and so help the unemployed, make taxation fair and provide industry with much-needed funds or nurture the illusion that a competitive industry and over-generous welfare are compatible.

5   Business and the labour market

Historical overview

To a greater degree than in the USA and in most other industrialized nations, French industry has been characterized by 'Fordism', i.e. mass production as used by the Ford Motor Company in which work was divided into defined, discrete tasks requiring little training or qualification. Part of the explanation for this lies in the rural origins of much of the workforce (in 1945, over 30 per cent of the working population worked on the land). With the rapid, forced growth of industry in the post-Second World War period and the veritable exodus of the population from the country to the towns, it was the type of employment most suitable to untrained masses. The same period saw mass immigration, too, which again fuelled the same organization of work patterns in industry. Both demographic developments were underpinned by an interventionist state which, through a series of **grands projets**, nurtured shipbuilding, the steel industry, the railways etc.

This was the heyday of French industry, the Trente Glorieuses, thirty years of virtually uninterrupted growth between 1945 and 1975 which were abruptly brought to an end by the two oil shocks. All previous assumptions on which growth was based were swept aside and the ensuing new economic and social realities together with the introduction of new technologies, generated a need to produce in smaller quantities. This in turn required a more qualified, multi-tasked workforce and a different view and approach to training and the preparation for work.

In the world of education, the unions had been uninterested in any form of vocational and professional training in schools. Being fundamentally anti-capitalist, they viewed this as indoctrination. The state, on the other hand, was not concerned with paying for companies' training either and so schools remained neutral and by and large divorced from any notion of adapting to the needs of industry. Hence, even in 1991, of 800,000 young people leaving school, 120,000 had no qualification at all. Fifty per cent of the working population have less than the CAP (**Certificat** d'Aptitude Professionnelle, see p. 123), a situation which particularly hits the young, women and older workers. To be sure, there is a payroll tax of 1.3 per cent levied on all companies employing more than ten people which is earmarked for training purposes but still 800,000 out of a total of over 3 million are long-term unemployed (more than 1 year) with half of these being out of work for more than two years. As in the UK this has led to feelings of exclusion and marginalization, to the rise of a dual society composed of those with and without work and periods of considerable social disturbance (riots in Vaulx-en-Velin, Sartrouville and Mantes-la-Jolie in 1990–1). Even the *lycéens* protested in 1990, a movement partly inspired by the knowledge that the mere fact of 80 per cent of an age range taking the *baccalauréat* (the government's target for the year 2000) does not automatically ensure jobs.

Demographic trends

According to the national statistical office, INSEE, at 1 January 1988 the population was estimated at over 55.7 million persons, compared with 55.5 million in 1987, thus growing at a rate of 0.4 per cent, compared with −0.2 per cent in former West Germany and 0.1 per cent in the United Kingdom. The fecundity rate at 1.8 children per woman has dropped since the 1960s, but if this rate continues the population will grow to 58 million in 2000. As in Germany and elsewhere, the population is ageing, however: in 2000, there will be 15 million people less than 20 years old, 1.1 million less than today; 12–13 million aged more than 60, representing 2 million more; and one million aged over 80, compared with 680,000 in 1983.

The geographical spread will look different too, with 35–6 per cent of households living in rural communities, compared with 27 per cent at present. Taking the population as a whole, nearly 40 per cent will live in rural communities, contrasting sharply with today's 29 per cent.

The number of immigrants is also growing. In 1985, France had 3.8 million foreign inhabitants, 21 per cent more than in 1972 and representing 8 per cent of the total population.

Size of the working population

As unemployment has climbed inexorably over the past decade, this has been accompanied by an increase in the working population. Between the census of 1982 and that of 1990, the working population increased by 1.5 million, reaching a total of 25.26 million in 1990. Three main factors explain this increase: first, the number of people of 'working age' (15–64 years) coming onto the labour market (190,000 per year); secondly, the number of immigrants (19,000 per year compared with 6,000 from 1975 to 1982); and thirdly, the rapid expansion of the female workforce (46 per cent of those aged more than 15, 74.4 per cent of those aged between 25 and 54). Two phenomena, however, have considerably modified the growth in the working population. Whereas in 1982–3 less than one young person in three aged between 16 and 25 years was still in the education system, nearly one in two (45 per cent) was in full-time education in 1990–91. This drop in the number of the young employed, due to longer time being spent in education and to the development of youth training schemes for those leaving school without qualification, has hence removed nearly 800,000 young people from the labour market and points to the difficulties the young have experienced in France in finding employment. Secondly, the number of those retiring after 55 and particularly after 60 (the legal age of retirement in France) has also contributed to a slowdown in the growth of the working population. It would therefore appear that the bulk of employment is concentrated in the 25–54 age range at a time when there has been almost stagnation in the number of new jobs being created.

Structure of the working population

Six per cent (1.5 million) of the total working population are immigrants (30 per cent being Portuguese, 16 per cent Algerian, 12 per cent Moroccan, 7 per cent Spanish, 6 per cent Italian and 4 per cent Tunisian). Some 57 per cent are **ouvriers** (shopfloor workers) – those particularly affected by unemployment – and are mostly concentrated in the Ile-de-France, Rhône-Alpes and Provence–Côte d'Azur–Corsica regions.

Reflecting the way in which traditional patterns of work have changed, some 6 million people are in less than full employment. Amongst these are 1.2 million having what is sometimes called in French 'precarious' (*précaire*) forms of occupation, e.g. 209,000 temporary workers, 580,000 on fixed term contracts, 322,000 **stagiaires** (a *stage* being any form of training course) and 80,000 apprentices. In addition there are a little less than 3 million on part-time contracts. Fixed-term contracts now represent 75 per cent of hirings in companies employing over 50 people particularly in civil engineering, construction and agriculture. Only 25 per cent are converted into permanent jobs, the average length being 2–3 months. The biggest increase over the past ten years (+40 per cent) has been in those doing part-time work, now some 12.5 per cent of the working population: 85 per cent of such jobs are held by women, primarily in the service sector, with 80 per cent of the increase occurring at *ouvrier* and *employé* level in restaurants, hotels, banks, insurance companies and at cash-tills in shops.

Although part-time work is still increasing, particularly in the public sector and amongst women (24 per cent), France still lags a considerable distance behind the USA (16.9 per cent), Holland (31.8 per cent), Denmark (23.3 per cent) and the UK (21.7 per cent). The biggest rise in temporary employment occurred in the 1960s and 1970s, to such an extent that controlling legislation was introduced and in 1982 temporary workers were awarded much of the status enjoyed by full-time workers. This in turn caused a big reduction in numbers with the consequent disappearance of many agencies, without, however, any noticeable upturn in full-time jobs. Another surge occurred between 1985 and 1989, when numbers almost doubled but temporary work only affects some 1 per cent of the working population. Many temporary jobs suffer the pejorative term of **petits boulots**, particularly in service industries, doubtless due to the sense of service not being highly developed in France. Often politeness in such jobs is even seen as a sign of weakness and is sometimes considered to put people at a disadvantage, particularly when negotiating. Service often equals servitude in French eyes and hence the welcome received at reception desks in many companies still leaves much to be desired.

In terms of the overall structure of employment by sector, the tertiary sector (services) continues to take the lion's share which has increased from 55.8 per cent in 1980 to 66.8 per cent at the end of 1992. In thirteen years agriculture has lost 750,000 jobs and now represents only 5 per cent of employment (8.5 per cent in 1980). The construction and civil engineering industries account for another 7 per cent of employment but have lost 300,000 jobs since the early 1980s, 90,000 alone in the last two years. Industry accounts for no more than 21.2 per cent of total employment having seen over 1.2 million jobs disappear, again since the early 1980s.

The service sector has essentially sustained the level of overall employment having created a net 1.8 million jobs over the same period. The fastest expansion came in 1984–90 but 1991 and 1992 saw a virtual collapse with only 45,000 new jobs created. Shops, restaurants and financial services now show negative growth in terms of employment and in the services rendered to industry, which represented the most dynamic sector, jobs are also now being lost (see Table 5.1).

Unemployment statistics

Unemployment statistics vary according to definition and hence numbers unemployed in France go from between 2.7 and 2.8 million using the International Labour Office's method to 3,141,200 as of June 1993 (11 per cent of the working population, 12.5 per cent by the end of 1994), using the figures of the national employment agency, ANPE (**Agence**

Table 5.1 *Evolution of employment in five sectors*

Employment on 31 December	1979	1984	1987	1990	1991	1992
Agriculture	1,856,643	1,552,654	1,393,935	1,220,058	1,171,754	1,111,800
Building/civil engineering	1,854,926	1,556,490	1,566,589	1,635,040	1,599,459	1,544,000
Industry	5,886,792	5,292,625	4,942,536	4,977,378	4,835,043	4,710,200
Commercial tertiary	8,468,211	8,929,642	9,461,204	10,231,862	10,253,787	10,277,000
Non-commercial tertiary	3,654,952	4,008,080	4,266,122	4,296,559	4,442,545	4,562,600
Total employment	21,721,524	21,339,491	21,630,386	22,375,226	22,302,588	22,205,600

Source: INSEE

Nationale pour l'Emploi), which gives the numbers seeking jobs at the end of the month. It is the simplest and most widely known indicator and will be used here. But whichever indicators are used, the trends are quite clear: the rate of unemployment grew constantly until the end of 1984, stabilized in 1985, only to rise again gradually until the beginning of 1987. The ensuing boom saw a modest drop until the recession sparked off another acceleration, particularly in 1991 (increase of 10 per cent) and 1992 (even in Bull, Renault, Michelin, Thomson and Philips) resulting in a rate of unemployment higher than in most other industrial nations (see Figure 5.1). In a recent survey, 69 per cent of the French population cited unemployment at the top of their list of major concerns.

In addition, one other factor bedevils official statistics, that of the so-called **traitement social** ('social management') of unemployment, measures designed either to reduce the working population or to give some sort of status to the jobless. The various measures introduced by the government (TUC, CES) will be discussed later but it is pertinent here to give the overall figure of 1.9 million people who are covered by such treatment and which, if added to official figures of employment (ILO or ANPE), paint an even blacker picture, particularly when many schemes are known not to lead to any real chance of lasting employment.

Structure of unemployment

The rate of unemployment amongst the young in the 16–25 age range stood at 21.3 per cent in 1985, one of the highest of the industrial nations. In 1990 it had fallen to 16.6 per cent but since then it has again risen sharply to reach 20.5 per cent at the end of 1992. Indeed, the rise in unemployment since the onslaught of the recession appears to have singled out the young in France and points to the underlying past failure of the education system already mentioned to adapt to the changing requirements of the labour market.

Unqualified workers have represented the category most affected by unemployment since 1974 and this tendency has in fact worsened, with the rate of unemployment amongst such workers exceeding 20 per cent in March 1992. Similarly, and indeed linked to the previous fact, the unemployment rate of immigrant workers compared with that of French workers has dramatically increased since 1980 when it totalled 9.2 per cent as against 6.7 per cent; in 1992, the corresponding figures were 19 per cent and 9.5 per cent. The situation of the **maghrébins** (North Africans) is of particular concern, exceeding 30 per cent and, even more worrying, the picture is the same amongst immigrant children possessing French nationality. From this, it can be seen quite clearly that unemployment hits hardest those with few or inadequate skills.

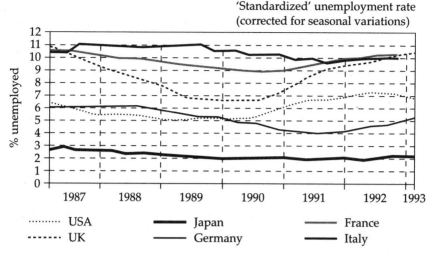

'Standardized' unemployment rate
(corrected for seasonal variations)

Figure 5.1 *Evolution of unemployment rate in large industrialized countries.* *Source: OECD*

Reference has already been made to the long-term unemployed whose number has increased constantly since 1979, with a brief respite between 1988 and 1990. Numbers stabilized in 1992 but only because the government focused its employment more particularly on this category. Paradoxically, however, the employment opportunities are more numerous than ten years ago but the new employment opportunities have essentially benefited those who have just left employment. Out of 3.7 million people hired in 1991, 1.9 million had come on to the labour market without being unemployed, 1 million had had no previous employment (students etc.) and only 760,000 were unemployed.

In short, amongst the unemployed, the probability of occupying a job diminishes considerably as the length of unemployment increases. Turnover amongst the unemployed is increasing, then, but it passes by the long-term unemployed.

One phenomenon is quite new, the unemployment rate of *cadres*. Although still only 3.7 per cent in 1989, the rate increased sharply by 34 per cent in 1991 and stood in July 1993 at 6.1 per cent, with central staff posts most affected (computers, personnel, design and research).

Great bitterness and anguish have been the result, particularly amongst the *cadres* who had thrown themseles into the fashion of company culture, plans and projects when in the 1980s the image of the company was rehabilitated as the creator of wealth and hence jobs, after decades of being mistrusted and living in the shadow of an all-providing state. The *cadres* had considered themselves apart from other categories of workers and certainly more or less immune from redundancy. Part of the problem is due to the increase in the overall number of *cadres*, particularly through internal promotion (*cadre-maison*). The axe has fallen most heavily in the service sector which employs 40 per cent of the cadres and which has suffered two-thirds of the job losses in this category (see Figure 5.2).

The business schools (**Ecoles de Commerce**) are beginning to feel the knock-on effect, as increasing numbers of graduates find that companies are no longer outbidding each other for their services. Fixed-term contracts of 6 months are becoming the norm, as at Framatome, the nuclear reactor constructor, where 300 such contracts – on lower pay – are currently on offer, a move which, if generalized, could well undermine the well-established French practice of **stages**, 3 months' job experience which students of both business and engineering schools regularly enjoy in each year of study. Belying the oft-heard complaint of a shortage of engineers in France, hardest hit are electronic, electrical and aeronautical engineers who once could expect red-carpet treatment.

Causes of unemployment

Although France has had a reasonable growth record over the past ten years and has indeed fared considerably better than the norm, it has consistently failed to create as many jobs as its competitors. Indeed, the present situation is such that an annual growth rate of 2.0–2.5 per cent is required just to contain unemployment but only with a rate in excess of 4 per cent would any dent be made in the rate of unemployment.

As elsewhere, the world recession took its toll, particularly the high interest rates necessitated by the government's *franc fort* policy within the ERM dictated by the Bundesbank in a Germany, racked by recession in the aftermath of its reunification. But other, specifically French, factors are at play, too, the foremost of which is the cost of labour. As has been seen, unemployment weighs particularly heavily on the unskilled and low-skilled and therefore, wages being the principal element of the cost of labour, there seems to be little doubt, according to a recent Banque Paribas report, that the existence of the minimum wage, the SMIC (**salaire minimum inter-croissance**) is acting as a brake on the ability of those seeking to enter or return to the labour market. In effect, it is pricing out low-paid low-productivity jobs and increasingly raising the barrier to entry. Crucially, the SMIC has risen faster (98 per cent in real terms between 1970 and 1992) than the average wage, whereas unskilled labour productivity has not increased as fast as the labour force average. In July 1993, the SMIC was received by 8.6 per cent of the private sector workforce and paid at an hourly rate of 34.85 francs, giving a monthly total of 5,889.65 francs for 169 hours.

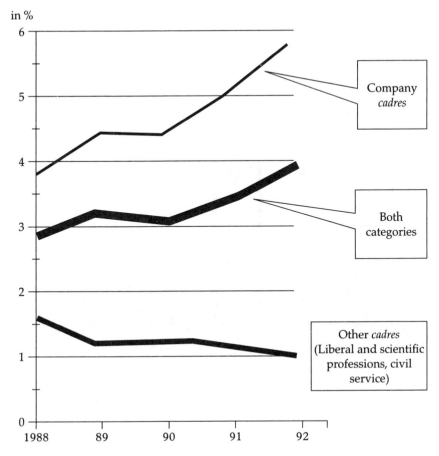

Figure 5.2 *Cadre unemployment. Source: INSEE*

Apart from wages, social charges (or National Insurance contributions) also add to the cost of labour and in France, because they are levied in such a way that as benefits or the numbers benefiting increase so do social charges – each scheme (sickness – URSSAF, pension – ARRCO, unemployment – UNEDIC) having notionally to balance its books – they represent a prohibitive cost and hence an increasingly onerous tax on jobs. Even contributions to pay for family allowances are borne by companies (although this is being phased out and transferred to the national budget in 1994). Between 1970 and 1990, whereas central taxes actually fell from 18.4 per cent of GDP to 16.4 per cent, over the same period social security payments rose from 13.1 per cent to 20.3 per cent. Compared with France's major competitors, only in Italy are non-wage costs per worker as a percentage of total wage costs higher in manufacturing (Figure 5.3).

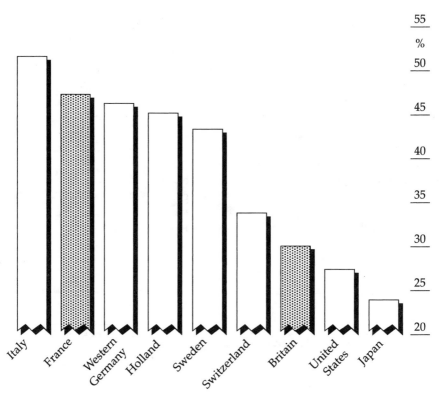

Figure 5.3 *Social costs. Non-wage costs (benefits including health care, pensions and insurance) per worker as a percentage of total wage costs, manufacturing, 1991. Source: German Economic Institute*

A third element of the cost of labour is the cost of the constraints imposed by the regulation of the labour market, overseen by local labour inspectors (**inspecteurs du travail**) to whom companies must submit regular statistics and information, ranging from numbers, age and gender employed to hours worked and minutes of the meetings held by the various statutory elected bodies. In addition, numerous registers covering rest periods, out-workers, even tips are required in law. But these duties have already been assumed by companies and new hirings would only therefore represent a marginal cost. It is, however, the obligation to draw up tightly-worded contracts for most full- and all part-time, temporary and out-workers, together with their associated rights, and the legal working week (39 hours) and statutory paid leave (five weeks per annum) which cause employers to calculate carefully the cost of hiring. And these costs can be considerable for those on permanent contracts. Redundancy pay, the right to a retraining course and a trial period in a new job whilst being retrained are amongst the most onerous. Redundancies in France rarely take the form of summary dismissals (**licenciement sec**) but are usually preceded by consultation with the appropriate internal bodies, e.g. the works council (*comité d'entreprise* or *délégué du personnel*) after a **plan social** has been drawn up (under the watchful eye of the local Inspector of Labour) detailing possible measures which might avoid or limit the number of such redundancies or provide for reclassification elsewhere where redundancy is unavoidable. Even voluntary redundancy schemes must be included for negotiation, since a change in the law on 29 July 1992.

Such a highly-regulated labour market leads to abuse, however, and there are an increasing number of cases where companies 'bend' the law, either to defraud the state through making bogus claims or to remain in business in a harsh environment. The general belief is that the law is changing constantly, that deregulation is increasingly apparent and therefore a company may only be just ahead of changes in the law in its practices. In theory, the labour inspector must be informed or makes his own checks, but in practice the labour code is so complex and far-reaching that there are insufficient resources to enforce the law. Officials often turn a blind eye when unemployment may be a consequence. Practices range from taking on young staff studying for a specific professional qualification and giving them totally unrelated jobs to do, for which companies are exonerated from social charges, to both falsifying overtime or compelling workers to do overtime or else lose their jobs. Employers, employees, local councillors, even members of parliament all connive at these and numerous other breaches of the law and unions are powerless, even unwilling to act.

Another structural cause of unemployment peculiar to France is the lack of sufficient small and medium-size companies (*petites et moyennes entreprises* – PME) creating jobs in both manufacturing and service companies. Indeed, since the watershed year of 1991, more jobs are being lost than created in the PME (2.5 million companies employing 0–500, with 93 per cent of French companies falling in the 0–10 range and only 2 per cent of PME employing 200–499). During the years 1988–90, before the reversal of the present trend, the PME created 985,000 jobs with 865,000 of these being in companies of less than 200 employees, particularly in sectors such as services offered to companies (computing, market surveys, training etc.) and hotels, restaurants and cleaning.

The low mobility of labour resulting from a complex system of house-buying finance and the deep roots many workers have in their regions also add to unemployment. For example, two-thirds of the 45–60 year olds live less than 20 km from their children. A recent report by the CNRS (Centre National de Recherche Scientifique) showed that in the greater Paris region (Ile-de-France) 30 per cent of adults had parents or parents-in-law and 60 per cent at least one child in the same *département*; 30 per cent live in the same area, 12.5 per cent the same street and 7 per cent the same building.

Finally, as has been seen, the lack of adequate training, coupled with the bad image of manual work leading to actual shortages in some industries, is a major cause of unemployment (also see Chapter 8 on training, education and development).

In spite of the hurdles to be cleared and the heavy penalties often incurred, redundancies continue apace and remain the government's top priority. In state-owned companies, a *plan social* is obviously required and in some cases, as recently in Thomson, rejected by the government as inadequate. This has not prevented wholesale job losses in these industries, however, and there are predictions of considerably more in overmanned companies such as Bull, Thomson etc. In the private sector, an interesting debate is developing in which a number of captains of industry have publicly voiced their serious concern at both the present level of unemployment and the speed at which redundancies are occurring. (Collective redundancies – **licenciements économiques** – were up by 17.8 per cent in 1991–2, totalling 485,000 in one year alone.) Many believe this smacks of hypocrisy on the part of those very people responsible for unemployment but it is indicative of the wave of fear overcoming all sectors of society, particularly of a social explosion if nothing is done to curb what is seen in many cases as excessive job losses. Indeed, the government has even threatened leaders of industry with increases in unemployment contributions if nothing is done to set their house in order. It has stopped short, however, of intending to bring back the control over redundancies scrapped in 1986.

There is no shortage of ideas on ways to combat unemployment. The young unemployed are to be particularly targeted, increasing the number of temporary work schemes (**contrat emploi-solidarité – CES**) from 450,000 to 650,000 over the next year. Like their predecessors, the **TUC** (**Travaux d'Utilité Collective** – schemes employing the young in the public sector such as on the Paris metro, the railways etc.), the CES are criticized for purely massaging the unemployment figures, the *traitement social* mentioned earlier whereby thousands are erased from the statistics at a stroke.

The German model of training has long been admired in France, as have so many other features of Germany's economy and industry, and hence another proposal is to double the number of full apprenticeships to 400,000 over five years, with the starting age cut from 16 to 14 years. This is again a hardy perennial but France has signally failed to engender much enthusiasm for apprenticeships, particularly in industry, no doubt due again to the poor image of the blue-collar worker. The cost implication for companies deters many, although the employers' federation, the **CNPF (Conseil National du Patronat Français)** backs the idea.

As part-time work (**temps partiel**) is relatively underdeveloped, it is seen by many as the panacea, particularly in the service sector, which has stemmed the tide of losses experienced in industry by the creation of part-time jobs. Eighty-five per cent of all part-time jobs are held by women, especially in domestic-related services. As more and more women reach full-time senior management positions and the population ages, it is forecast that the demand for such positions is likely to increase considerably. It is often confused with another idea, that of shared time (**temps partagé**), whereby work is spread around more people but with less pay as the sting in the tail. Pay cuts have also been suggested and indeed implemented in such companies as Potain and Publicis to save jobs. Originally, the government ingenuously offered to subsidize such pay cuts but when a number of companies started to use this as blackmail, the idea was quickly shelved. A reduction in the working week is back in favour, too, in spite of evidence concluding that very few jobs were created when the last reduction to 39 hours was introduced by the previous Socialist government in the early 1980s.

The service industry is also looked to for more job-creation. A recent report for the Plan, the Brunhes report, suggested there should be a real industrial policy for services, a sector it considered rich in potential jobs. Too much priority, it stated, has been given to automation which has steadily eroded such jobs as petrol-pump attendants, metro drivers and ticket-collectors. The Japanese are seen as the model but nowhere is it clear who exactly will foot the bill, although exemption from social security contributions is seen as one way of making such a scheme viable. Claude Bébéar, the influential head of Axa, one of France's largest insurance companies, argues that maybe levels of productivity have gone too high. In Axa, the emphasis is on part-time work, particularly for women, who represent 60 per cent of the workforce in the Paris region. With more flexible timetables (400 already do not work on Wednesdays, a day-off for schools in France), it is estimated another 200 jobs can be created. For its *cadres*, the company has other original plans such as forming a reserve of *cadres* aged over 50 who will not take early retirement but will continue to receive a salary, but at a reduced level. Their services will be called upon in times of crisis or shortage or to act as trainers, when they would be employed again on full salary.

In another service company, Pierre et Vacances, in the tourist sector, seasonal workers are to be given the status of full-time workers with their salaries averaged out and paid throughout the year, even when inactive. In the largest and state-owned chemical company, Rhône-Poulenc, 1,000 extra young people will be taken on in exchange for those over 56 accepting to work part-time.

Many other similar schemes exist, each one adapted to particular circumstances in a labour market, which is highly segmented and regional by nature, and therefore has to escape from the straitjacket of blanket national measures. These suggest that the causes of unemployment are identifiable whereas the creation of a special commission by influential industrialists within the Institut de l'Entreprise has as its objective to leave no stone unturned in its search for a clear and realistic vision of what is seen to be still fundamentally unknown territory, littered with half-baked economic truths and preconceptions, particularly where the influence of productivity, technology and relocation of labour are concerned.

At national level, the government has drawn up a five-year plan which has, as one of its main thrusts, a change in the Code du Travail, the whole raft of labour laws which lays down a comprehensive legal framework for every aspect of employment. For example, it is proposed that working hours should be annualized rather than rigidly counted weekly without resort to overtime and layoffs (39 hours being the legal working week, before overtime is paid up to an overall ceiling of 48 hours). If annualized, workers' rights (e.g. to do overtime), under the Code will therefore be more subject to company requirements arising from the rhythm of operations, a position hotly contested by the unions. Similarly, in spite of strong union opposition, certain sectors such as banks may be allowed to modulate their work schedules, enabling them to open six days out of seven provided workers are allowed two consecutive days rest, one of which must be Sunday. At present, the law requires banks to close on Monday, if they wish to open on Saturday.

With the aim of reducing the cost represented by legal requirements concerning worker representation in companies with less than 100 employees, functions such as those exercised separately by staff delegates (*délégués du personnel*) and works committees (*comités d'entreprise*) could be amalgamated with frequency of meetings reduced. Social security costs could also be reduced by the gradual shifting of the burden of family allowance contributions from companies to the state, starting with salaries less than 1.5 times the minimum salary and gradually extending to higher salaries over five years. Exoneration from social security contributions will be continued for the creation of up to three new jobs, as also for fixed-term contracts of at least 12 months. The untouchable SMIC emerges relatively unscathed, however, but a recent report on employment, the Mattéoli report, recommends that future adjustments could well be limited to linking to inflation only and not also, as in the past, to annual increases in purchasing power equal to half that of the average working wage. The government seems likely to balk at such a measure, however, as it would strike at the very heart of one of the most cherished *acquis sociaux*, those rights and privileges enshrined in labour law and so zealously preserved in France.

Short-time working will also be extended, involving state aid to avoid redundancies by paying 50 per cent of gross salaries for up to 1,200 hours spread over a maximum of eighteen months. Short-term contracts can be renewed twice up to 24 months, where previously it had been 18 months. In the domestic services area, a **chèque-service** is proposed whereby individuals could buy, say, a coupon for 150 francs in a post office or bank, which when handed to someone wishing to act as domestic help, for example, would represent a payment of 100 francs. The balance would represent social charges and would have to be accounted for by the issuing organization. The essential objective of this measure is to remove the labyrinthine steps which need to be taken by the individual employed to register with the URSSAF, the social security managing authority.

In the area of youth training, the regions will increasingly be more responsible, with apprenticeships proposed from the age of 14 onwards. Training 'spaces' are also planned for all workers throughout their working lives. Long periods of training will also be able to be taken 'for personal reasons'.

Changes to legislation covering Sunday work are also envisaged, highlighted by the much-publicized fines (and handed over to trade unions!) imposed on Virgin for opening its Megastore in the Champs-Elysées on a Sunday. The original law of 1906 restricted such work to continuous-process industries and to certain small food shops, cafés, hotels, flower shops, museums etc. The latest modifications of 1992 allowed the *préfet*, on a regional basis, to grant temporary and renewable permission to certain shops to open in 'tourist areas', the definition of which has led to much heated arcane debate. For example, do Juan-les-Pins and Golfe-Juan rely more on a seasonal influx of visitors than their bigger neighbour Nice and, if so, should back-street shops be allowed to open in the former but not in the latter? In global terms, some 4 million salaried workers in France are involved in Sunday working. To these must be added another 2.5 million non-salaried independent workers, which includes shop-owners, who in many areas can open their shops as long as they do not employ salaried workers to help.

Immigrants and the labour market

By far the largest group are those from the Moslem countries of North Africa – Algeria (780,000), Morocco (520,000) and Tunisia (212,000) – although there are considerable numbers of Portuguese (860,000), Italians (425,000) and Spaniards (380,000). Although many will have entered the country quite legally, mostly after 1945, a considerable number were illegal, a situation which particularly suited employers who could thus pay lower wages, hire and fire at will, and pay less attention to working conditions.

Many of the original immigrants also arrived without their families, hoping to find a job and save up enough money to go home and set up in business. The majority stayed in France and were later joined by their families (as was also to be later the case with many illegal immigrants who regularized their position). Thus family groupings are on the increase, with women representing 38 per cent of the Algerian and Tunisian population. More than 80 per cent of immigrants in France today have residence permits and work permits valid for ten years, but automatically renewable.

The bulk of the immigrants arrived in France without qualifications and took jobs on building sites, as unskilled workers on assembly lines, particularly in the car industry or the less salubrious jobs, such as emptying dustbins, which the French disdained to take.

With the onslaught of *la crise*, many immigrants were the first to suffer, representing two-thirds of redundancies in the construction industry and the greater part of the massive lay-offs in the car industry, particularly of Talbot, in 1983. Today, more than a third of them are to be found in local grocery stores or as waiters in cafés and restaurants.

The immigrant is often the first to be laid off and the young often leave school with few qualifications and hence find it difficult to find jobs. For the older ones, reconversion is difficult, at times impossible, as many are still unable to read or write French. This led to the failure of plans to reconvert Talbot workers and miners recruited directly in the Atlas mountains.

In the Ile-de-France region, 30 per cent of the long-term unemployed are immigrants and hence in 1977 the government introduced its first plan to encourage immigrants to return home. Some 60,000 – mostly Portuguese and Spanish – took advantage of the scheme between 1977 and 1982, and in 1980 50,000 Algerians benefited from a special Franco-Algerian agreement to provide travelling expenses and training centres in Algeria. The scheme was revived in the car industry in 1984 but, after some initial success, rapidly ran out of steam, most immigrants viewing acceptance of aid to return home as acceptance of failure and preferred to stay in a country in which they are not always welcome. Racial friction often erupts as the French accuse them of taking their jobs, committing the majority of crimes and of forming ghettos. Islam is now France's second religion and this alone is a source of much tension, particularly over the claim to the right for girls to wear the traditional Islamic head-scarf, the *tchador*, in schools – anathema to the highly anti-clerical teachers' union which jealously protects a lay state system and brooks no recognition of religious affinities. Islamic fundamentalism is taking a firm grip in the Algerian education system and many see the *tchador* issue as being a fundamental exercise in surreptitiously spreading Islamic propaganda. The numbers of immigrants is still being swollen, too, by illegal entrants who prefer indignities at the hands of unscrupulous employers to poverty in their native lands.

The situation of ethnic minorities came even more sharply into focus in the early 1990s with the resurgence of the National Front, under its leader Jean-Marie Le Pen. Once thought to be a spent force after an initial ignominious attempt to become president, he is now recognized as representing the forces of disaffection, and many apparently respectable French would not disagree that his beliefs have some appeal. His success was such that, on immigration issues, the other political parties began to echo his sentiments, in a shabby attempt to win more of the popular vote. Of overriding significance to the French is the EU's stance on immigration. Tougher all-round policies which can be implemented in neighbouring countries, through which illegal immigrants easily pass, are seen as a key element.

Conclusion

Chirac has decided to play for high stakes. By making employment his priority but without any real means to support his intentions, he risks political fallout if he fails. Whatever he decides, he has no real power over companies which alone hire and fire and who are waiting for a shift in macro-economic policies such as a drop in interest rates (often termed the 'British solution' in France). And the pious utterings and beguiling suggestions of leading industrialists are belied by their actions when market conditions dictate drastic measures, including redundancy. Through it all, the country is slowly being divided into two camps: those in work with all the accumulated rights and privileges accorded by an all-embracing and inflexible Code du Travail and those without, for whom the former are not prepared to forgo their rights in the name of solidarity. This is the paradox in France, where so many are preoccupied by unemployment yet unwilling to tolerate any tampering with the legal edifice providing them with protection. Flexibility is the great unknown which might provide a solution but in a country keen to avoid uncertainty.

6 Business and trade unions

The conflict which came to a head in Air France in October 1993 again provides an example rich in lessons, trends and developments in business in modern France – this time in the sphere of industrial relations. First, the resulting strike occurred in the public sector, the traditional bastion of trade union membership and influence. Second, the dispute was marked by violent militancy, a form of unionism which has long been the hallmark of union action in France. Third, in spite of union involvement, however, the pace of the strike was set by **la base**, the rank and file which in recent years, often in the form of 'coordination' groups, has tended either to bypass or dictate to official union channels in public sector strikes. Fourth, the survival plan proposed by the new head of Air France, Christian Blanc, was put as a referendum, over the heads of the unions, directly to the whole of the 40,000 workforce.

This chapter will examine these four points by looking at the extent of union membership and influence, together with the movement's strengths and weaknesses, the policies and strategies of the different confederations of unions and the process of collective bargaining in France.

Trade union membership

Standing at 9.6 per cent (1993) of the workforce, union membership in France is by far the lowest in the European Union. There is nothing new in this, except that the rate of decline has been more dramatic, decreasing from a membership peak of 28 per cent in 1982 to its present low point in the late 1980s, a development which has affected all unions. Male membership has dropped from 29 per cent to 15 per cent, female from 11 per cent to 7 per cent. Precise figures are notoriously difficult to obtain, however, since paying union dues by a monthly deduction from salary is not legal, there being no equivalent of the UK check-off system, whereby members authorize such payments. There is some difference of opinion over how many months' dues must be paid to qualify for membership. Payments are at best irregular, with six per year being the average. There are variations by sector, too, with the highest percentage (20 per cent+) being in the public sector and between 6 and 8 per cent in private companies.

One fundamental reason for low membership is to be sought in the origins of the unions. From the very start they espoused a policy of having a core of militants whose task it was to encourage demonstrations and strikes for political reasons rather than concentrate on organizing a mass stable membership. Such a revolutionary stance, however, existed long before the official recognition of unions in 1884. Until then, all forms of corporations and professional associations had been banned by the **Loi Le Chapelier** of 1791 which had ushered in a long period, therefore, of clandestine activity which impregnated the mentality and practices of militants. In the nineteenth century the labour movement witnessed three mass uprisings which were brutally suppressed in the name of public order in the Revolution of 1830, the *canut* (silkworkers) revolt of 1848 and during the Commune of 1871. Each one added to the revolutionary culture of the 'vindictive' workers who inspired fear into the bourgeoisie, with their violent tracts distributed in the workforce and still fresh memories of the Revolution of 1789.

Such powerful folklore dies hard – the Commune was tearfully invoked by a survivor at the CGT congress in 1935 – and even during the Air France violent conflict, constant nostalgic reference was made to the uprising of 1968, accompanied by the refrains of the 'Internationale' and a certainty that militancy would be revived. Revolution and anarchy were the starting point of modern-day trade unionism in France, then, as opposed to any form of institutional integration into a political party and a mass movement which would seek a progressive, more or less peaceful negotiation of improvements in salaries and working conditions through collective bargaining. The class struggle, and anti-capitalism, were the watchwords which find echoes even today in labour relations in France. Such an ideological stance, however, has cut little ice with the workforce the unions are deemed to represent, in that workers' individual interests come a poor second. With the demise of communism, in particular, dogma is dead for all but a few militants.

There has been no unity of ideology either. Indeed, the history of the union movement in the twentieth century is one of schism after schism, of one splinter group after another in a highly complex patchwork of factions, tendencies and sections. Fragmentation has resulted from internal strife and fuelled yet further the disenchanted frustration of workers.

If workers have shunned ideology, employers, too, have been less than enthusiastic about a labour movement which struck at its very vitals and only reluctantly accepted legal recognition of union sections in companies as late as 1968. Lack of any established presence in the workplace was thus another reason why unions failed to attract members, especially in small companies of less than fifty employees – which employ more than 50 per cent of the total workforce in France – where even today membership is considerably less than in large, particularly public sector, companies. Even when their presence was legalized, French unions did not enjoy the same privileges as their counterparts in other European countries. The closed shop, for example, was officially banned although in reality it is alive and well as a practice amongst dockers and print-workers.

Another disincentive to membership has to do with the way in which collective bargaining agreements are made. Agreements made at a national industry level between unions and employers may be 'extended' in certain circumstances to employees, whether unionized or not in companies not belonging to the employers' association signing the agreement. Employees see little reason, therefore, for membership of unions when they are covered anyway by the terms of such agreements. The scope of extended agreements has been strengthened in recent years, thereby exacerbating this reaction even further.

Economic, social and industrial developments, particularly in the 1980s, have also taken their toll on declining numbers in unions. The demise of smoke-stack industries (steel, coal etc.) employing masses of unionized labour has been a significant factor, as has the concomitant increase in the number of jobs created in small companies where, as we have seen, unions have traditionally had no real presence. The increase in so-called 'precarious' forms of employment, part-time, temporary etc., has not aided the unions' cause, particularly in the service sector. One section of the workforce which has increased dramatically in France since the 1970s has been the technician grade (BTS, DUT) and, here too, the unions have signally failed to galvanize attention and interest. Against this backcloth of changing employment patterns and qualifications, of economic turmoil, industrial upheaval and end to security of employment, and, above all, of the loss of the old seemingly unassailable 'truths' represented by communism and socialism, the unions have lost their way and clearly failed to formulate policies more in keeping with both employees' economic aspirations and the reality of global competition.

Indeed, the major union confederations have bickered even more amongst themselves; so great is the divorce between the nostalgic yearning for the unchallenged certainties of a golden age of confrontation and disputes and the perplexing speed of present-day economic and social change in which no clear path is obvious except compromise, adaptability and realism, all of which go very much against the grain of the heavily bureaucratic and rigid French union movement. Lack of financial resources, in turn a consequence of low membership and low dues, is a final barrier to any large-scale promotional attempt to attract greater numbers and to provide alternative services to members (insurance, reduction in prices for certain goods and services, etc.).

The major confederations

The title of 'union' when applied to the five largest unions is really a misnomer, since in reality they are each a confederation of unions, in turn constituted in a complex mix of either industrial or craft federations. Traditionally, these confederations are both 'horizontally' and 'vertically' organized – horizontally across industries which have local and regional organizations grouped geographically, and vertically in that these geographical organizations are represented in one single national body. In addition, the confederations have particular sections organized along workforce sector lines, e.g. *cadres*, engineers, technicians etc. In 1991, for example, the CGT (**Confédération Générale du Travail**) had 34 industry federations and two national syndicates (journalists and atomic energy workers), FO (**Force Ouvrière**) had 35 federations, CFDT (**Confédération Française Démocratique du Travail**) 20, CGC (**Confédération Générale des Cadres**) 80 and CFTC (**Confédération Française des Travailleurs Chrétiens**) 48.

One of the most important features of the five major confederations is their 'representativeness'. They are automatically recognized by law as representative of various categories of industry, trade and employee at national level for the purposes of collective bargaining agreements (**conventions collectives**). This right was conferred on them in the 1950 Act using the criteria of the number of members, their independence from employers, fees, experience and their patriotic attitude during the Second World War. Representativeness also gives other privileges in the constitution and voting of certain internal officials and bodies in French companies (see below, Statutory internal representation in French companies).

Confédération Générale du Travail (CGT)

In its early years, the CGT, formed in 1885, epitomized the strain of revolutionary anarchism running through the French trade union movement in its belief in direct action, tough strikes, anti-capitalism, but also anti-militarism and anti-religion. A crucial event in its history was the formulation of the **Charte** (charter) **d'Amiens** of 1906 in which, notably, it declared its firm strategy of the general strike and its independence from all political parties and the state. The latter was to become of particular importance in ensuing years as it led to constant internal splits over the gradual erosion of its original stated intention of remaining autonomous. The development of the CGT became increasingly linked with that of the French Communist Party (**PCF** – **Parti Communiste Français**) which believed in using the CGT as its 'transmission belt' (*courroie de transmission*) to achieve its political objectives through conflict in the workforce. In 1985, the executive committee was made up of ninety-five communists and thirty non-communists, but even more telling is communist influence at the vital departmental and regional levels where dominance is almost total. Such an overt allegiance to a party still committed to marxist doctrines even after the collapse of the Soviet Union has no doubt caused the greatest individual decline in the membership fortunes of the trade unions, with a 50 per cent drop recorded in the 1980s alone to its present level of some 1 million, although some commentators put it as low as 500,000–600,000.

The first split occurred after the First World War between the Communists and the 'reformists' who were in favour of some form of 'collaboration' with state institutions. The rift was healed under the Popular Front of 1936 when strikes led to the employers' acceptance of the Matignon agreement, which must be seen as the first landmark in what was to become increasing intervention by the state to legislate in labour relations often in the aftermath of confrontation (echoes of the UK in the 1980s), as opposed to employer–union collective bargaining agreements. Under the Matignon agreement, there was a general increase in salaries, and the introduction of the 40-hour week, paid holiday entitlement and the *délégués du personnel* (workers' delegates). At that time the CGT numbered some 5 million members. Under the Vichy government, all confederations were banned and most went underground to play a powerful role in the Resistance movement in the struggle against collaboration and occupation, although again not without splits in the CGT between the Right and Left elements. Harmony was restored in 1943 only to be broken again in 1947 over the continuing pre-eminence of the Communist Party. Ranks were closed again in opposition to the forming of the Fifth Republic and during the successful miners' strike of 1963.

Since the 1960s, the CGT has been presided over by two powerful figures, Georges Séguy (1967–82) who tried to revive class struggle unionism and to pursue a course of unity with other unions and Henri Krasucki (1982–92) who had to contend with two presidential terms of Mitterand, the demise of the Communists, the collapse of the Socialists and also of union membership. His was the delicate task of 'critical support' of a Socialist government which did not prevent the CGT from taking militant action in support of steelworkers, in the long-running dispute with the Swedish ball-bearing manufacturers SKF in Ivry and eventually to a hardening of attitudes towards the Socialists. More recently, in the late 1980s, the CGT has reaffirmed its policy of confrontation by favouring listening to *la base* and getting involved in emerging conflicts. It sided with the Communist presidential candidate in 1988 and with Communist MEPs in European elections, thus underlining that its marxism has survived intact the fall of the Berlin Wall and the collapse of the Communist regimes. It participates guardedly in national collective bargaining since it believes resulting agreements may well erode social legislation. Its particular numerical strength is amongst skilled manual workers in engineering, local government and health, and in the construction and chemical industries. Fifty per cent of its membership is in the public sector.

Confédération Générale du Travail – Force Ouvrière (CGT–FO)

Generally known as FO, its full title is revealing in that it points to the split which occurred in 1948 as a result of a faction of the CGT, the founders of FO, which disagreed with the dominance of the Communists within the CGT, invoking the 'Charte d'Amiens' principle of independence from all political party influence. It also underlines the tension still felt within FO between the desire to continue with the 'old CGT' and to affirm a new realism. Under André Bergeron (1963–89), FO became the preferred link between both Georges Pompidou and Valéry Giscard d'Estaing and the labour movement. Although Socialist in beliefs, it remains determinedly independent of the Socialist party and because it refused to become involved in government policy, its membership increased during the 1980s. With its new and less popular president Marc Blondel, FO hardened its attitude towards the governments of Cresson and Rocard, particularly over public sector pay policy and, latterly, it has reviewed its position over the use of strikes, especially in its internally divisive concern not to allow the CGT a monopoly over militant action, a position which again stresses the continuing antagonism between and within the various confederations. It would seem that, within this context, the days are over for the earlier policy of a reconciling *'unité d'action'* programme on which all unions could agree and promoted particularly by CFDT and FEN. Traditionally, FO has been strongest amongst white-collar workers and technical and professional groups in the public sector but it has strenuously courted the private sector which has seen the biggest increase in membership. Unlike the CGT, FO sees legitimate advantages in collective bargaining and one reason for the recent increase in its popularity is undoubtedly the way in which it has been seen to further workers' interests through its willingness to negotiate. In spite of a drop in numbers in 1990 and 1991, FO remains the union which, in popular opinion polls, best meets with employees' aspirations in its moderation in spite of references to the 'class struggle' in its policies and being culturally close to the CGT. Indeed, it can be seen to be one of the FO's weaknesses that it tries to be all things to all men and consequently suffers on occasions from all too familiar internal strife.

Confédération Française Démocratique du Travail

After the First World War a Confederation of Christian Workers was formed which eventually split into the present **Confédération Française**

des Travailleurs Chrétiens (CFTC) and the CFDT, which severed its official confessional links and thus ended any reference to 'Christian' workers. It underwent a period of radical policies between 1966 and 1977 (it played an active part in the 1968 riots and promoted a policy of **autogestion**, a form of worker control), only to review its strategy and subsequently cease both to profess itself Socialist and to seek the end of capitalism. Its stance has been markedly reformist under first Edmond Maire and Jean Kaspar since 1988 in its belief in the benefits of negoti-ating contractual agreements. Present policies include support for priva-tization, small and medium-size companies (*petites et moyennes entreprises* – PME) and a public sector pay policy, thus establishing its credentials as a modernizing anti-corporatist confederation. Much of the thinking behind the Lois Auroux, to be discussed later, was inspired by links between the CFDT and ministers in the early Socialist government cabinet. Jacques Delors, the previous president of the European Commission, was also close to the CFDT, whose ideas he has used to promote a 'Social Europe'. It is strongest in engineering, the health sector, the oil and chemical industries and in banking and insurance.

At present, the CFDT is recovering from a management crisis in which Jean Kaspar was asked to be replaced as general secretary by Nicole Notat, who, unlike the CGT and FO, who were openly hostile to Balladur's policies, particularly those expounded in the quinquennial employment plan of October 1993, has adopted a policy of systematic, but not neces-sarily negative, criticism of the government. For this reason, it is well regarded by the government, especially in its willingness to criticize the sense of *avantages acquis* gained back in the Trente Glorieuses. Its basic policy is therefore job creation for the have-nots rather than protection of the privileges of the haves. Unity with the other unions, although preached in the early 1990s, is now being questioned, given fundamental differences between the CFDT and the CGT and FO.

Confédération Française des Travailleurs Chrétiens

Originally formed in 1919, after prompting by the Vatican in the late nineteenth century for a Christian movement to counteract the effect of Freemasonry, the CFTC, after the creation of the CFDT in 1964, was reconstituted principally by miners from the strong Catholic area of Le Nord. It has undergone the same soul-searching as the other major unions and, like them, has suffered membership losses particularly through mine closures. Its main numerical strength is amongst teachers in private schools (its present president Alain Delen is one such teacher), in the health sector and in the food industry, and in banks in Alsace, Le Nord and Paris, although it has no real presence in companies. It sup-ports non-politicization of unions, collective bargaining, a ban on night and Sunday working and is strong in the co-administration of the Caisse Nationale des Allocations Familiales.

Confédération Générale des Cadres (CGC)

Originally excluded from the CGT because they were seen as the holders of delegated power, *cadres* (see Chapter 8) eventually formed their own confederation, the CGC, in 1944, made up of three former unions founded in 1937, in a flourish of union activiy in the aftermath of the Popular Front. Engineers, too, had formed separate unions at the turn of the century which were either Catholic or Freemason in inspiration.

Between 1944 and 1963, although encountering difficulty initially in being recognized as a 'representative' union organization, because of the presence of known 'collaborators' amongst its members, the union became the dominant influence amongst *cadres*. In particular, it was concerned with championing a special pension scheme for *cadres* within the *Sécurité Sociale* (all *cadres* belong to the general scheme – **régime général** – but, above a certain ceiling, also subscribe to an obligatory additional scheme – **régime complémentaire**). In the early 1960s, the CGC's monopoly began to be eroded with competition from *cadres* sections formed in the other main confederations. A split occurred in its ranks in 1968 over the desirability or not of wage differentials and this was followed by yet more conflict, often physically violent, in 1978. With Mitterand's government in 1981, there was protest over the levelling of salaries and what was seen to be the attempt to 'Sovietize' companies with the **Lois Auroux**, the inspiration of a government which then had a number of communist ministers. Protests against the government ended under the prime ministership of Fabius when the CGC embarked on a new policy to be more constructive, particularly in multi-industry negotiations. Nevertheless its membership dropped by one-third between 1976 and 1986, even though it now appeals to a broader category of employees, e.g. sales representatives, supervisors and technicians.

Autonomous and independent unions

In French companies many other organizations enjoy union status but are not nationally recognized as being as 'representative' as the big five and are therefore not included in industry-level collective bargaining agreements. They do have a set number of hours allocated to them for official business and they are allocated premises. They also have certain negotiating rights under the Code du Travail (Labour Code). If none of the five big confederations are present in the company, any other union must prove its representativeness for negotiating and internal voting purposes, if necessary in a court of law, if contested by the employer or another union.

The autonomous and independent unions do not have the same expertise or wealth of relationships as the big five and hence many become affiliated to the larger confederations. They represent all forms of employee and their spread extends from Members of Parliament (*députés*) and journalists to lorry drivers, railway workers and *concierges* and *gardiens d'immeuble* whose union is close to the extreme right-wing party, the **Front National**. The largest is the union representing those working in education, the **Fédération de l'Education Nationale** (FEN), which is typified by a completely arcane web of currents and undercurrents and of numerous short-lived factions.

As will be seen, the existence of independent groups represents a constant and growing threat to the representativeness of the major confederations in elections to key internal positions and bodies.

Statutory internal representation in French companies

The numbers employed by a French company are a critical issue, since much that is required under the Labour Code is triggered off by various threshold levels. Training is obligatory in all companies employing more than ten, for example; for those exceeding 100 employees, a special reserve must be formed for profit-sharing (**participation aux résultats de l'entreprise**) and a **bilan social** (showing employment trends and salary) is required of companies of more than 300 employees. A collective bargaining agreement can bring these levels even lower.

As far as employee representative bodies are concerned, the important thresholds are eleven and fifty, at which points a **délégué du personnel** (employee representative) becomes necessary for the first and a **comité d'entreprise** (works committee) for the second, together with a **délégué syndical** entitled to 10 paid hours for union work for each representative union. The duties of the *délégué du personnel* are to present both individual and collective claims to employers, covering salaries, the application of the Code du Travail, of health and safety regulations and of any collective bargaining agreements relating to the company. Election of these *délégués* is by two rounds of voting with unions having the priority in proposing candidates in the first round. This principle reinforces the view that in practice in labour relations in France the unions do enjoy considerably more influence than their low membership figures suggest. Most *délégués* are elected on a union platform, whether that of one of the big confederates or one of the independents. Employees are then said to be **sympathisants**, i.e. they agree with the unions to the point of electing a union representative but without seeing any point in being a member. But in spite of the obligation to have *délégués* in companies above a certain size, in reality a recent report found that in a clear majority of small firms employing between eleven and forty-nine they just do not exist.

This raises the whole issue of the validity of having a detailed legal framework for labour relations which, in practice, companies can and do flout with apparent impunity in France. In a wider context, it highlights a fundamental cultural difference in attitude to rules and regulations which, if they cannot be enforced, tend to be viewed far more flexibly and casually than is the case in the United Kingdom and certainly in Germany.

The *comité d'entreprise* is elected in the same way as the *délégués du personnel*, with the unions benefiting from the same privileges. It must meet once a month with the head of the company as chairman who calls the meeting and sets the agenda. It must be informed and consulted over questions of employment, redundancies, research and development, the introduction of new technologies, profit-sharing schemes etc. The list is impressively long but in many companies, either they do not exist (30 per cent of companies employing 50–100) or, where they do exist, their role is generally seen as organizing Christmas parties, company outings and fishing competitions. Even in well-organized large companies, the popular image is of 'good works', an image often cultivated by the elected members of the *comités* who find it difficult to depart from their traditional role of being more concerned with vote-catching moves to foster employees' individual well-being than with more significant attempts to have a say in the company's business. Providing help for those under threat of redundancy has been seen as a legitimate cause for the *comités* to take up but, here again, old ideological reactions come quickly to the fore, as the unions hold back from being seen as aiding and abetting management decisions. Nevertheless, in this area too, as in a greater awareness of the economic realities of companies' activities, the *comités d'entreprise* are slowly having some impact in companies where they are the first to alert employees to the company's difficulties and to turn anodyne monthly meetings into debate, suggestions for alternative strategies and even protest over measures taken. To be able to discuss such matters intelligently they receive extra resources to employ experts to advise them, a measure introduced by the Lois Auroux in the early 1980s.

Another innovation of these laws was the introduction of *groupes d'expression*, in which employees have the right of direct expression over working practices and conditions. Both managers and unions alike were quick initially to express their opposition, but where they exist, they are the result of company-level negotiations involving the unions, with whose *délégué syndical* the management must discuss how they should be constituted and operate. Such groups have now waned in popularity, as have quality circles (which by law they must not replace, although they may co-exist) largely because they are increasingly seen to be going through the motions and not effectively dealing with employees' requests and complaints.

One other organization worthy of note, external to companies but crucial to the unions' ability to gain wider support (**audience**), is the **conseil de prud'hommes**, the industrial tribunal or 'labour court' which is composed of two employer and two employee representatives, the latter being elected along the same lines as the *délégué du personnel* and *comité d'entreprise* as regards the priority accorded to union candidates. They number 279 in total and are responsible for deciding on levels of compensation after wrongful dismissals.

The decline in support for unions, with a concomitant growth in popularity of non-union candidates, can be seen in the figures for *comité d'entreprise* elections (see Tables 6.1 and 6.2). By far the biggest crisis has been suffered by the CGT whose percentage of votes fell from 37.4 per cent in 1977 to 25.1 per cent. The other unions have fared considerably better, stabilizing and even increasing their share but the biggest rise has been in the non-union vote from 18.8 per cent in 1977 to 26.4 per cent in 1989. In *conseil de prud'hommes* elections, the proportion of votes gained by unions has remained steady, but again with a decline in influence of the CGT (Table 6.3). Overall, however, the elections of 9 December 1992 showed a growing indifference to their importance by employees.

At national level, too, unions have representatives in around 100 public organizations which give them a wider political and social role, particularly in those bodies connected with the running of the welfare state, i.e. pensions, unemployment and sickness benefits. These are managed on an equal basis between employer and employee representatives and include UNEDIC (for unemployment benefits), ARRCO (non-*cadre* pensions) and AGIRC (*cadre* pensions). The system for reimbursement for medical treatment (**Caisse Primaire d'Assurance Maladie**) and for family allowances (**Caisse Nationale des Allocations Familiales**) are similarly managed, thus allowing unions a considerable say in the level and allocation of benefits and providing another example of how the weakness implied by low membership is belied, this time, by influence in organizations strictly outside the field of labour relations. Other important institutions in this respect are the **Commissariat au Plan,** which consists of a number of sectoral commissions whose task is to collect and analyse data for preparation of the five-year economic plans which were started after the Second World War, and the **Conseil Economique et Social**, an advisory body to the government on economic and social questions. At *département* level, the unions also have representatives on some thirty committees. The existence of union representatives, however desirable they may be from a union point of view in developing the

Table 6.1 *Results of works committee elections (%), 1977–1989*

	CGT	CFDT	FO	CFTC	CGC	Others	Non-union
1977	37.4	20.2	9.0	3.0	5.4	5.7	18.8
1979	34.4	20.5	9.7	3.1	5.8	4.8	21.2
1981	32.0	22.3	9.9	2.9	6.1	4.1	22.2
1983	28.5	21.9	11.1	4.0	6.5	4.7	22.8
1985	27.7	21.2	12.6	5.0	6.2	5.8	21.5
1987	26.8	21.3	11.3	4.8	5.9	6.0	23.9
1989	25.1	21.0	11.2	4.6	5.5	6.3	26.4

Source: Liaisons Sociales, 25 July 1990

Table 6.2 *Results of works committee elections as a percentage of seats obtained, 1987*

CGT	CFDT	FO	CFTC	CGC	Others	Non-unions
18.3	15.9	9.1	3.6	5.1	4.6	43.6

Source: Liaisons Sociales, 23 February 1989

Table 6.3 *Elections for industrial tribunals (% of the vote)*

	CGT	CFDT	FO	CFTC	CGC	Others
1979	42.3	23.2	17.3	7.2	5.2	4.8
1982	37.0	23.5	17.7	8.5	9.6	3.7
1987	36.5	23.0	20.4	8.3	7.4	4.5

Source: Bibes and Mouriaux, 1990

myriad of *avantages acquis* so fiercely defended, particularly by the CGT, does point to a central question: is the numerical weakness of the unions attributable to precisely this wider state-engineered representation at institutional level, since employees see no need for membership of an organization which, with or without their support, exercises influence? Even more fundamental is the issue of union strategy and whether this representation is seen as a compensatory factor for low membership or whether, in reality, the unions would prefer to have a strong mass base, too, in order to have more influence directly in the workplace. This leads directly to the need to look at the role of collective bargaining in labour relations in France which hitherto, as in so many other aspects, has been atypical when compared with other European countries.

Collective bargaining agreements

Many major social advances came via the state under the Popular Front of 1936 and after the liberation in 1946, but there were also contractual agreements, i.e. directly between unions and employers such as the Matignon (1936) and Grenelle (1968) agreements. It has been an issue central to labour relations practices in France how far the state should play a role in legislating as opposed to greater emphasis on collective bargaining agreements (**conventions collectives**), particularly at plant level in circumstances in which neither unions nor employers were authoritative, the unions because they feared erosion of *avantages acquis*, the employers because they were hostile to the unions. Indeed, the Lois Auroux (1982) must be seen in this context in that they were an attempt to stimulate contractual practices with less intervention by the state.

Provision for such bargaining was made in the Act of 1919, which did not distinguish between company and national level. Few companies were inclined to discuss directly with the unions, anyway. There was a flourish of company agreements in 1936 but the pendulum swung back to national bargaining being favoured in the 1946 Act. One of the biggest changes in the industrial relations scene of the 1980s, however, has been the way in which the company has become the heart of contractual activity, where previously agreements had been made more often at industry-level, a situation which had suited both employers, because of their lack of enthusiasm for unions in the workplace, and unions, because they were able to negotiate improved salaries and working conditions agreements which would then cover even those companies where they were poorly represented. Such national negotiations are still very much a feature of contractual agreements, however, being by law obligatory every year for wages, and every four years for job classification.

Between 1983 and 1990 the CFDT and CFTC signed the greatest number of agreements at company level, with CGT, FO and CGC signing less (see Table 6.4). Salaries and working time have been the most common themes, followed by changes in technology, qualifications and training, although the latter three areas have been of much less concern. In 1992, the number of company agreements fell by 6 per cent but covered more employees due to the greater involvement of large companies. Often company agreements are adaptations of industry-level agreements to specific corporate requirements, e.g. on salaries, provided that the increase in the total wage bill is at least equal to the national increase and that minimum rates are requested. This, together with negotiations on more flexible working time, has been increasingly seized on by companies as an opportunity to be less restricted by rigid national agreements, thus bringing them more into line with contractual arrangements existing in other countries. In companies employing fewer than fifty, negotiations

Table 6.4 *Evolution of number of company-level agreements between 1983 and 1990 and rate (%) of signature by unions*

	1983	1984	1985	1986	1987	1988	1989	1990
No of company/site agreements	2,278	4,076	5,165	6,778	6,484	5,085	5,793	6,496
Signing organization								
CGT	59	53	52	49	48	45.9	47.8	45.4
CFDT	49	49	49	48	49	49.6	49.0	50.4
FO	36	41	42	41	40	40.3	49.0	40.0
CFE-CGC	40	40	40	39	41	40.1	38.9	38.4
CFTC	14	18	18	18	18	18.0	17.5	19.2
Divers	13	11	11	11	12	11.2	10.7	14.0

Source: Bilans annuels de la négociation collective, Documentation française

leading to agreements are, however, still rare (5.8 per cent of agreements in 1990), thus underlining the importance for the unions of the 'extended' national bargaining agreements. Such agreements are extended by the Ministry of Labour to those companies falling within a given sector as identified by an elaborate series of code numbers (which figure in a company's registration number for identification purposes) issued by the national statistics office INSEE (**Institut National des Statistiques et Etudes Economiques**). A company knows whether it is covered by these agreements by referring to the codes for its sector.

At the top of the list of those unions signing national agreements stands FO, with the CFDT and CGC showing the biggest increase in inclination to sign. The CGT is some way behind, as with company agreements which it still views as a company subterfuge to do away with the cherished *avantages acquis*.

In addition to specific industry-level agreements there are also multi-industry negotiations which deal with unemployment, training and working conditions. In the early 1980s, these were questioned by the CNPF, who doubted they had any real value but they still exist to lay down general guidelines which may be adapted to a company or industry. At European level, too, the unions take part in discussions with the employers' organization UNICE on the same issues at Val-Duchesse. Within specific companies such as Bull, Thomson, BSN and Elf, the European dimension has also had an impact with the creation of *comités de groupe* (group committees) to allow contact with unions in other countries.

A final form of consultation is worthy of mention – the referendum, which was used most spectacularly at Air France but for which there were precedents at Thomson, Potain, Taittinger and Publicis. This was a direct appeal, over the heads of the fourteen wrangling unions, to the workforce to accept the latest in a long line of survival plans. Each department was also consulted, managers were written a personal letter asking for ideas and 2,700 working groups were set up to make suggestions. This direct consultation of the employees has made a forceful entry into the field of labour relations in France as a result of the weakening of the deeply-divided unions unable to compromise in a business world where more sacrifices than liberties and *avantages acquis* are required from responsible partners. Interestingly, such moves as the use of a referendum have not been denounced by the unions for fear of being disowned by those they are deemed to represent. Indeed, in some cases it has been the unions who have been in the forefont of the demand to use such means.

Overall, in collective bargaining, the unions are confronted with a double problem. First, they are doubtful about the utility of engaging in talks which are often called by the employers or the government and end in union capitulation. Second, more and more companies are beginning to question the validity of signing agreements with organizations which are so marginally representative of the workforce and, just as importantly, with no guarantee of peace.

Strikes

Strikes are a fundamental right under the Constitution of 1946. During a strike, the employee's contract is merely suspended and therefore no salary is payable. Certain types of strike are illegal, the **grève perlée** (staggered strike, with one department going on strike after another), the **grève du zèle** (go-slow) and the **grève de solidarité**, although they regularly occur in practice. No previous secret ballot is required, but notice of five days is required in the public sector. **Piquets de grève** (strike pickets) are permissible but must only, officially, exercise **réprobation silencieuse** (silent protest). Physical or moral pressure is illegal. A **grève sur le tas** (on-the-spot strike, with employees staying in the workplace) is not illegal since only temporary and occurring during work hours. The frequently used **occupation de l'entreprise** (sit-in) is illegal because it goes beyond working hours but usually action is not brought by the employer since conflict is usually resolved by the promise of withdrawal of such action!

Overall, strikes are steadily declining but the number of local and short stoppages is still significant, although the number of days lost in France is still considerably less than in other EU countries. In 1992, 500,000 individual working days were lost through strikes, the lowest figure since 1946. Some larger strikes have hit the headlines in the recent past, however, particularly in the public sector amongst tax inspectors, prison warders, nurses, and at Renault. In the case of civil servants, in spite of a guarantee of virtually lifelong employment, the basic reason has been the stagnation and erosion of salaries since the 1980s, at a time when yet higher qualifications are required. In the main, however, long strikes are unusual since union funds are limited, due to low dues, and therefore in general strike pay is not given. The CGT is the union particularly associated with mass demonstrations involving the mobilization of large numbers and sees such action as being as much a part of its tradition as any other form of activity such as collective bargaining.

Many strikes are now led by **coordinations**, groups which are often spontaneously formed by *la base* (rank and file) outside the union movement. The CGT has decided to work with such groups, often jumping onto the bandwagon to control the action, but the FO has expressed great distrust of such *coordinations*, particularly where they involve violence and disruption such as that perpetrated by the fishermen and lorry drivers. In the case of the farmers, the recent outbursts of protest against reform of the Common Agricultural Policy and the signing of the GATT agreement was organized by the Coordination Rurale in direct opposition to the main farmers' union which was considered to be taking too soft a line with both the national and the European authorities. Both the CGT and the CFDT played an important supporting role to *la base* in the Air France conflict as it brought back memories of militant days. '*Ça rappelle '68'* (it brings back 1968), one CFDT *délégué* said, and it was time to remind all French of *'une tradition de lutte et de résistance'* (a tradition of struggle and resistance). But it was *la base* which basically dictated the pace and direction of the action; *'c'est la base seule qui jugera de la reprise du travail'* (only the rank and file will decide on a return to work), in the firm belief in their democratic legitimacy and strength which cut across all hierarchical considerations. *'La base pense que'* (the rank and file think that); *'la base n'est pas d'accord'* (the rank and file do not agree); these were common statements amongst a movement which considered the strike to be 'its' strike, its 'movement'. *'On se moque des étiquettes, des engagements, et de l'appartenance de tel ou tel à un syndicat. On est tous ensemble dans la même galère'* (We couldn't care less about labels, commitments, and about so-and-so belonging to a union. We're all together in the same boat). The reaction of the unions was highly revealing: *'On accompagne, on soutient, on suggère une démarche, on donne quelques informations en notre possession, mais en aucune façon on ne mène'* (We go with them, we give support, we suggest making this or that move, we give information in our possession but in no way do we lead).

Although the **patronat** (employers) must share the blame for the weakness of the unions, most employers view the action taken by spontaneous,

often non-unionized and therefore uncontrolled *coordinations* with considerable trepidation, as with new technology and different working
practices and organization it is comparatively easy for a small group of
individuals to cause major disruption.

Conclusion

Labour relations at Air France, then, sum up much that is typical of
labour relations in France in general: a plethora of squabbling unions,
very little support and trust shown from the rank and file which often
takes the law into its own hands and finally a state which intervenes
as it has throughout the history of the labour movement. New forms of
more direct appeal to the workforce as a whole are appearing such as the
use of the referendum.

Although the violence and destruction of the Air France stoppage has
been echoed on a number of occasions in the past few years, strikes on
a grand scale orchestrated and strictly controlled by the unions are a
thing of the past. Old traditional conflicts have become anachronistic,
such as those at the watch manufacturers Lip in 1973 and at the engineering company Manufrance, also in the 1970s. If *la base* shows no reaction in a spontaneous outburst, then often the response is that which
occurred at SKF in 1993 where employees looked on, petrified of retali-
ating, as colleagues were sacked within the hour and sent home by taxi.
The unions, too, stood by and accepted the reality of the moment. Give
in fearfully or react spontaneously – often not to prevent job losses, but in
a corporatist attempt to preserve *avantages acquis* – are now the options.

But in one important aspect, French unions have come to resemble
more those in other countries as the onus of negotiation has gradually shifted away from industry-level collective bargaining agreements
to company-level agreements, with the state holding more and more
aloof from legislative intervention. A once-reticent *patronat* has realized
the greater flexibility of tying company agreements to the reality of their
individual competitive performance, and unions, with the exception of
the CGT, are beginning to take a more realistic view of their role, faced
with virtual decimation of their membership. Nevertheless, the unions
have much to do as they struggle to change the image they have in the
public mind of revolutionary unions with a long history of combative
struggles and strikes. The Fordist organization of workers now being
outdated, they are faced with a highly diverse workforce whose interests
they struggle to understand, yet alone represent. Internecine warfare still
abounds as the unions find themselves far removed from forming the
equivalent of a TUC, so split are they over new strategies and policies to
adopt. When a major union, the CGT, refuses to accept there is a crisis,

when the FO hovers between protest and compromise, the CFDT is in the grips of a management crisis as a new figure, Nicole Notat, emerges to replace Jean Kaspar and the FEN is literally exploding, the future for French unions looks bleak. Other countries' unions, too, have fared badly, but in France the decline has been sharpest against the backcloth of a low membership in the first place.

One sign of hope on the horizon, however, was the importance which the previous prime minister, Edouard Balladur, attached to having a stronger, more responsible union movement, ready to discuss what are difficult, sometimes taboo subjects: job classifications, mobility, training, work organization, cost of labour, union rights, etc. Balladur was particularly in favour of more union involvement in the management of the Sécurité Sociale, although here the unions are already hesitating since the introduction of new regulations requiring employees to work a greater number of years and pay more contributions to be eligible for their pensions. More *concertation* is proposed, too, between the government, employers and the unions but the unions are unwilling to be seen to be conniving with decisions taken. Participation, General de Gaulle's grand idea, is back in favour but CFTC and CGC are in favour, CFDT is hesitant and CGT and FO are adamantly against.

Hope there may be, then, but the unions' capacity to disagree is as yet more powerful than their sense of urgency.

7 Business and employers' organizations

Introduction

On 13 December 1994 the main employers' organization, the **CNPF (Conseil National du Patronat Français)** elected a new president, at a time when France awaited the election of a new national president, due in the spring of 1995. The latter was of particular significance for the CNPF, since one of the two main candidates for the post of president, Jean Gandois, who retired from Péchiney, firmly believed that to keep abreast of competitor countries France needed a number of fundamental and pressing reforms which could not be undertaken until a successor to Mitterand had been decided. The CNPF should be committed, he believed, to playing a firm leading role in formulating proposals for reform, particularly as the employers' organization was in need of strengthening its image and sharpening its focus which were severely dented and criticized on all sides as the recession deepened. The CNPF is no stranger to opposition but as the economy is liberalized and international competition intensifies, with companies increasingly being under greater scrutiny both at home and abroad, it faces yet another challenge to the image of the company. Record levels of unemployment and charges of corruption at the highest level of the Establishment have cast long shadows over the legitimacy of firms and those who lead them.

Historical background

In the early nineteenth century, companies were family affairs only interested in making a profit, which was then systematically reinvested to make yet more money.

Products were thus expensive and to maintain high price levels, employers were not prepared to brook any form of competition and hence formed associations to defend their interests, even though officially these, like trade unions, were illegal. The silk makers created a union of textile manufacturers in 1830, the linen and cotton makers followed suit in 1837 and 1839, and in 1832 the sugar beet producers in Northern France combined their efforts to combat the introduction of cane sugar. The 'forge masters' set up a committee in 1840 to defend the interests of the metallurgical industry and this led to the **Comité des Forges** in 1864 which even into this century had such a powerful influence over both the industrial and political scene.

Such associations and committees essentially encouraged agreements which led to cartels, dividing up markets or price-fixing. Crucially for the future of industrial relations, the rich families controlling the companies were in no way interested in the economic advancement of society unless it suited their interests. If these were threatened, then obstacles were put in the way of progress. The reign of Napoleon III was a golden age for industry. A more enlightened view of the role of industry was promulgated by Saint-Simon, who believed entrepreneurs engaged in production were the key to the future economic prosperity of society, but also emphasized the well-being of workers. This was the hey-day of engineering. Much of France's emphasis, in the period following the Second World War, on state-led industrial sectors managed by Grandes Ecoles which produced engineers and administrators devoted to the cause of an enlightened state, derives directly from the thinking of Saint-Simon. In the 1860s the big fortunes of such families as Schneider and Wendel in the metallurgical industry and Kuhlman and Deutsche in chemicals were made as the upper middle-class grew into a powerful intermarrying caste of the '*deux cent familles*', that small band of families which well into the twentieth century held the reins of industry.

In 1919 the first interprofessional employers' organization, the **Confédération Générale de la Production Française (CGPF)**, was founded with the initial purpose of defending itself against state capitalism, after the war period in which the state took a leading role in organizing industry for the war effort. It consisted of twenty-one federations formed according to trades with committees to coordinate the activities of the different federations. It was essentially a pressure group which attempted to influence government policy. The Comité des Forges continued to exist however, as did the **Union des Intérêts Economiques**, founded in 1910, to defend the interests of industry.

Industrial relations were typified by widespread paternalism on the part of the employers, who made contributions to employees' weddings, children and holidays but were totally opposed to any form of negotiated salary increase. The **maître des forges** was alone, after God, responsible for his company and those working in it and embodied the figure of the 'father', an image which the French had great difficulties in overcoming. The recognition of the right to form a union in 1884 was absolutely rejected by the employers, a refusal which led to bloody strikes and generally the employment of harsh methods to break up unions. Such deeply-ingrained hostility to the workers left its indelible mark and significantly contributed to the uncompromising revolutionary syndicalism of the embittered unions. This open hostility came to a head in 1936 with the election of the left-wing Popular Front, headed by Léon Blum. The victory of the left led to an explosion of strikes not only to extract higher wages but also to force recognition of the unions and worker representatives in the PME (*petites et moyennes entreprises*). The resulting Matignon agreements were the first of the major state-prompted agreements at national level described in the previous chapter on trade unions and were followed by laws introducing far-reaching benefits for workers. The 40-hour week, 15 days' paid leave and improved collective bargaining were introduced in a clear victory for the workers, but a humiliating defeat for the employers who rounded on the CGPF delegates and attempted to limit the new workers' rights. Militant union activists were sacked, and in many cases employers refused to negotiate under the new conditions.

Blum's departure in 1937 went some way to placate the big employers but the PME remained implacably hostile to the workers, since the full cost of the Matignon agreements fell on the smaller enterprises. They suspected, too, that they were the victims of a plot by the large companies to destroy them as competitors and this hatred of both workers and the so-called 'trusts' led to calls for a more authoritarian regime, no doubt providing fertile breeding ground for extreme right-wing tendencies. Under the Vichy government, the CGPF was dissolved and gave way to **comités d'organization** (organization committees) charged with organizing production in the war economy. Many of the members of the CGPF were heads of these committees and to the workers' hatred of the Vichy regime was soon added contempt for their employers who were regarded as the least patriotic by public opinion. Although the line between collaboration and keeping the company ticking over (*'il faut faire tourner la boutique'*) in the interests of survival was often very thin, there is little doubt about the depth of hostility felt towards employers, particularly by the unions, so much so that the National Resistance Committee demanded widespread nationalization at the end of the war. The present CNPF was set up in December 1945 with the intention of bringing together large and small companies, in both industry and commerce. It acted as the employers' representative commission to de Gaulle, who himself expressed great contempt for employers, summed up in his oft-repeated question '*Où étiez-vous, messieurs?*' (Where were you, gentlemen?)

In the 1950s, the CNPF had a clear vision of the importance of transforming an agricultural, protectionist and deeply conservative France into an industrial France with a key role to play both in Europe and the rest of the world. For many employers, the change was dramatic. The loss of independence involved in acceptance of the Iron and Steel Community was viewed with some trepidation and the conviction that once borders were open, French industry would fall into the hands of the Germans. The 1950s also saw the creation of a new young employers' organization, the **Centre des Jeunes Patrons** (CJP), which was inspired by radical catholicism and the Saint-Simonian philosophy in its belief that employers were morally responsible for the welfare of their employees. Profit was not only to the benefit of the family owners and shareholders but was to increase the wealth of the workers. For the CNPF this was still too radical and it was not until the Paris riots of 1968 that it began to change its views. Also, during the 1950s, a grocer called Poujade led a movement which attempted to persuade the state that it had a duty to subsidize small businesses, particularly shopkeepers. It gave rise to the idea of **poujadisme**, the protectionist, anti-competitive tendency which marked the formative years of the Common Market and has remained an underlying theme in France. The **Loi Royer** limiting the number and size of hypermarkets was also the result of a similar movement started by Gérard Nicoud following the events of May 1968.

In the 1960s, the **énarques** took over the economic machine completely in France at a time of great prosperity and strong growth. Politicians were of little importance as the technocrats forced the pace, backed by the power of the Planning Commission. Even then, however, the CNPF was plagued by its abiding and still present weakness: it was a heterogeneous pyramid of many interests, ranging from the PME to large companies. Consensus and compromise were hence difficult to achieve and resulted in debilitating conflict. Fortunately, however, it had a colossus at its helm in the person of François Ceyrac, the president from 1972 to 1981, considered to be the golden age of the CNPF, as it developed a significant contractual relationship with the unions. Its title was the subject of fierce and significant debate in the late 1970s, with the large companies preferring to substitute the word *entreprises* for *patronat*, which was considered to be too off-putting and divisive. They believed the CNPF should be shown, through its title, to be defending the whole company and not just the employers. The PME won the day, however, who felt under severe attack both from the unions and the government's Sudreau report on labour relations and believed a change would be tantamount to giving in to pressure and going soft, particularly on the unions. Strife between employers and unions was at its height, as Mitterand's *programme commun*, a common political platform with the communists, sowed both panic and loathing in the employers. Ceyrac was constantly at loggerheads with Mitterand at a time when the word *'syndicalisme'* was particularly powerful, signifying that employers and unions belonged to one entrenched camp or the other, according to their vision of society. In the USA and Germany, the vision of society is generally accepted on all sides. In France, it was capitalism or its revolutionary alternative. Even today, the English word 'syndicate' needs using with some caution in France, being so highly charged with emotive undertones in the context of labour relations.

The *'patrons'*, then, were caught between the two extremes of the overwhelming superiority complex of owners by divine right and the feeling of being rejected by the community, of being unloved and despised. If they succeeded, they were exploiting the workforce. If they failed, they were incompetent rogues. The unions, on the other hand, particularly the CGT, were out to *'casser la baraque'* (smash up the dump, i.e. the firm). French capitalism was deeply impregnated with the statist and syndicalist traditions, with, on the one hand, an omnipresent, authoritarian state, and, on the other, the marxist demagogy of employees. State authoritarianism had its counterpart in the absolute monarchy of the PDG (**Président-Directeur-Général**), who rejected all notion of compromise with the worker rabble and typified the Napoleonic military tradition that, to lead an army, one mediocre general was better than two exceptional generals.

If the 1970s witnessed the thawing of an intransigent CNPF, in spite of the despair at the end of the decade born of the continued, even growing, hostility of the unions spurred on by prospects of victory of the Left, the 1980s saw a radical sea-change in companies' image. The whole vast experiment of the early years of the new Socialist government which came to power in 1981 under Mitterand's presidency failed catastrophically and, in 1983, the Socialists were forced to execute a spectacular U-turn by freezing prices and incomes, tightening exchange controls and increasing taxation, including a compulsory loan. Many jobs created in the state sector were precisely those to go first. Perhaps the greatest sign of the true significance of the U-turn was the new-found belief by the Socialists that only companies, not the state, could create wealth and therefore jobs. The image of business was rehabilitated and was no longer the subject of scorn and mistrust. In parallel, trade union membership fell rapidly and the dominance of marxist 'truth' declined, particularly in the latter half of the decade. But the CNPF has not been able to capitalize on the profound changes and was even deeply divided in 1986, with a right-wing government in power, over the extent and nature of liberalizing the economy and the role of the 'social partners'. As with the unions, splits are endemic and the CNPF continues to be accused of inertia resulting from an excessive search for unanimity. Behind the scenes, it claims to have played a crucial role in engineering greater levels of competitiveness of French companies, strengthening companies' equity, obtaining lower corporation tax and encouraging a gradual shift to private pensions. In the eyes of the general public, however, the CNPF is a weak institution which is no longer listened to or consulted in social and economic debates. Sharpest criticism comes from the government which accuses it of lack of commitment and compliance, particularly in the fight against unemployment. In return for a drop in social charges, the government expects an effort on the part of companies to limit redundancies. Although right-wing, it believes companies can 'control' employment but the CNPF remains resolutely independent in its contention that it cannot dictate to companies and that only an economic upturn can create more employment, not less taxes *per se*.

With a new national president, it is likely that France will emerge from its *attentisme* and confront some of the major reforms it needs, particularly the balance between a level of social protection and a flexible labour market. It remains open to conjecture whether a new CNPF president will be able to channel the disparate strands of the organization into an effective and powerful consensus. As in the past, it seems more likely that powerful individuals at the head of state-owned or newly-privatized companies, members of the tightly related politico-industrial seraglio, will have more decisive influence with government. Winning the hearts and minds of the public, however, will be difficult for the CNPF against the background of unemployment and recent cases of corruption.

Membership

Out of 1.5 million companies, only a few hundred pay up regularly as direct members of the CNPF. Direct membership is mainly through narrow professional federations, of which there are ninety, and employer multi-industry 'unions' (**unions patronales**), which number 150.

The dues paid by the federations and unions represent 90 per cent of the CNPF's income (110 m Ffr in 1993). Companies belong directly to the federations and unions, some of which, particularly in the case of the latter, wield considerable local power. Many are trade organizations as well as employers' associations, active in promoting members' economic interests as well as playing a bargaining role in industrial relations. There is a separate organization representing the PME, the CGPME (**Confédération Générale des Petites et Moyennes Entreprises**) which is jointly represented with the CNPF in the *prud'hommes* (industrial tribunals) but is otherwise quite separate from the CNPF. The Lois Auroux of the early 1980s were the main cause of the separate paths taken by the two organizations. Lastly, the SNPMI (**Syndicat National des Petites et Moyennes Industries**) is a more extreme institution, quite prepared to stoop to violence, if necessary.

Chambers of Commerce and Industry

Because they play a leading role in local and regional business life, the **Chambres de Commerce et d'Industrie** (CCI) must be mentioned. The

CCI date back several centuries over which time they have considerably added to their original functions. Purely in financial terms, their influence and activity are considerable, in that they are financed by an obligatory tax paid by some 1.5 million employers, who also elect their representatives. In the public mind, they are particularly associated with establishments run by the CCI – the airports in Nice and Lyon, the top business school, HEC (Hautes Etudes Commerciales) in Paris and various ports around the coast.

They were legally constituted by an Act of 1898 and represent the commercial and industrial interests of all industries and services in a certain catchment area. This is in contrast with the employers' federations and unions, which speak for the narrow interests of one or a group of industries. In addition, unlike the employers' federations, they are public bodies, having buildings and equipment providing a public service. At local and departmental level, they are not alone in representing employers – two other organizations serve a similar purpose, the **Chambres des Métiers** (Craft Chambers) which represent craftsmen and the **Chambres d'Agriculture** for farmers. Again, these are public and non-sectarian.

In total, there are 160 local or departmental CCI (also called **compagnie consulaire**). In theory, there is at least one per *département* but as in the case of the Paris Chamber, one may cover several *départements*. In addition, there are twenty-two regional chambers (CRCI, **Chambres Régionales de Commerce et d'Industrie**), corresponding to the twenty-two administrative regions. This comprises representatives of each of the departmental CCI. Finally, there is the permanent assembly of the Chambers of Commerce (**Assemblée des Chambres Françaises de Commerce et d'Industrie**, ACFCI), which has as its members all of the departmental and regional chambers. Although the overall structure is pyramidal, the intention of the 1898 Act was to create bodies representing local interests and hence the chambers described at the various levels are totally independent of one another, although they may act in concert.

Although now quite independent from public authorities, the original chambers of commerce created during the reign of Louis XIV formed part of a rational network of organizations reporting to a central authority (the **Conseil Général du Commerce**) and capable of providing the king with information to enable him to formulate economic policy. They were also a way of controlling the local activities of fractious *bourgeois* merchants whose independence and economic clout were a source of some concern for the monarch. Unlike the newly-ennobled *bourgeoisie* (the so-called *noblesse de robe*), these merchants were uninterested in buying royal offices, the classic way of being elevated to a subservient aristocracy, but concentrated on developing their business. To keep them in check, members of the *noblesse de robe* were appointed as safe state-appointed functionaries to run the local chambers of commerce. As new towns were built, they were endowed with a chamber, including the town of Amiens which was the first, in 1761, to have representatives of industrialists as well as merchants.

During the Revolution, the Chambers were suppressed, being considered to be a form of 'corporation' and therefore covered by the Loi Le Chapelier, which proscribed the early forms of workers' associations. Gradually, however, albeit unofficially, the Chambers, especially those in La Rochelle and Marseille were re-established as it became clear that they contributed to the proper running of public infrastructure, and more particularly, to financing the economy through the raising of local taxes. With the arrival of Bonaparte, largely engineered by bankers and merchants, the Chambers of Commerce were officially re-established in 1802. Although during the eighteenth century they had become largely independent, under Napoleon they were extremely centralized, being placed under the strict tutelage of the *préfet*, whose task it was to ensure that they did not stray from their legal duties. These were, principally, to provide views on how trade might be increased, to inform the government of impediments to progress and to supervise the execution and running of public works which helped trade, e.g. ports, river navigation etc. With the Restoration in 1830, the Chambers of Commerce became truly independent as the victorious merchant and industrialist classes finally acceded to political power. The Chambers of Commerce can be seen, therefore, as having been an important element in the rise of the trading and manufacturing classes in France and they illustrate the constant tension between a tendency towards a high degree of centralization and a fierce determination to remain independent of the state.

Elections

One constant major theme in the evolution of the CCI has been the relative weight to be given to the various professional categories and to companies of different size. Much of the Poujadist movement in the 1950s was centred on the CCI where the essential tussle was over whether the vast majority of small firms should be able to impose their views on larger companies whose economic activity might be vital in certain CCI catchment areas. Many of the smaller firms represented (or underrepresented, as they claimed) were retailers, and hence in the 1970s there was a determined attempt to split the CCI into two distinct bodies, one for commerce and one for industry. A parliamentary bill to this effect was rejected largely on the grounds that both sides were interlinked activities and the CCIs gained their importance and relevance precisely through this complementarity. A bill was passed in June 1973, however, which made it impossible for any one of the three professional categories (commerce, industry and services) to obtain a majority of seats. A minimum representation of the smallest companies is also guaranteed.

Those eligible to vote must be at least 30 years old and be able to provide evidence of exercising a trade or profession for five years which has led to being registered on the **Régistre du Commerce** (Register of Commerce), on which registration is an obligatory formality to be able to conduct any form of industrial or commercial activity in France). In addition, the PDGs of *Sociétés Anonymes* are eligible, as are the first persons mentioned on the Registre du Commerce as responsible for the other forms of company, two additional representatives for SAs, SARLs and other forms of companies, a representative of a branch of a company established in the CCI's area, members of the industrial courts (**tribunaux de commerce**) and lastly civil airline pilots and ships' captains who are considered to represent their employer. Those CCI with more than 30,000 electors have 38–64 seats and those with less than 30,000 between 24 and 36. Election is now by one ballot for a single person, rather than a list, a system heavily criticized since it favours the election of local 'notables' in small and medium-size towns where the CCI together with the **mairie** (town hall) is a strong bastion of the local notability.

In spite of the very real power vested in the CCI, the turnout at elections is low, in the range of 35–40 per cent, a figure which has risen from barely 20 per cent before the Second World War, when such lack of support was seen to be largely due to the absenteeism of small companies. Voting increased in the 1950s with the rise of the Poujadist movement which threatened to take control of many CCIs. Their opposition to Algerian independence upset many of their followers, and the number of seats held by the movement declined rapidly. The vigour of the movement's activities did shake the CCIs out of a certain state of lethargy, however, and for a time the turnout at elections increased considerably, but only where there was real competition for seats, as in the early 1970s when a faction similar to the Poujadist movement in its aims, led again by a small shopkeeper, Gérard Nicoud, made its mark.

Because voting is so low, the true representativeness of the CCI has therefore been questioned on a number of occasions. The government would like to see participation exceed at least 50 per cent and changes to the law have allowed various associate members to take part in the work of the CCI. There has even been discussion of extending this to all *cadres* but as yet no decision has been made. As with associate members, they would only have a consultative role and would not be permitted to vote in elections. An interesting aspect of this move is the light it sheds on the battle between employers' organizations and trade unions to attract *cadres* to their ranks. On the one hand, the CCI can obviously see the value of coopting *cadres* but, on the other, their hesitation reflects their desire to be employers', not employees', organizations.

In one sense, the question of the low voting patterns is explained by the same reason put forward for low membership of the trade unions. In the same way that the benefits of collective bargaining agreements apply to all companies and all employees in a given sector, whether unionized or not, the activities and services of the CCI are available to all companies and therefore elections are seen as irrelevant.

Activities of the CCI

Because their precise mission is ill-defined, over the years the CCI have enlarged their functions away from purely one of consultation and representation, to controlling and managing infrastructure, services and organizations rendering services to their members. It is this latter activity which has largely gained more importance than the purely consultative role.

Consultation and representation

The government requests the CCIs not only to formulate opinions but the CCI also have the power to present their views on how to increase the prosperity of industry and trade. In fact, in a number of cases the opinion of the CCIs must be sought by law: regulations relating to commercial practices, the establishment of new *tribunaux de commerce, conseils de prud'hommes* etc., taxes to pay for public transport (a tax levied on the payroll of all companies employing more than nine people in towns of more than 20,000 inhabitants and yet another cause for complaint by the employers over excessive taxes and social charges), civil works contracts, e.g. motorways and particularly taxes or tolls to pay for them, labour rates in prisons. In short, any commercial, economic, legal, financial, social or fiscal matter may be commented upon or recommended by the CCI. Quite naturally, there is a great divergence of opinion amongst the CCI but their role in this case is to be seen as a primary filter of public opinion, in which local notables act as 'gatekeepers'. In reality, it appears that the public authorities take little note of the CCI's opinions but nevertheless they continue to insist on their consultative prerogative and not to be seen as purely administrators of public assets. At the level of the regional chambers and the national assembly of Chambers of Commerce, there is an attempt to synthesize opinions and present a more homogeneous front. Here, however, the main question is one of duplicating the work and views of the employers' professional organizations such as the CNPF and CGPME which enjoy more clout with the government than the CCI.

Lastly, within the context of the national Plans and their regional counterparts, the CCI are represented by law on numerous committees and commissions at both local and regional level on matters ranging from town-planning, education, taxation and social security to agriculture, tourism, historic monuments and transport.

Administrative and management functions

Dating back to 1898, the CCI have been authorized to build and administer such establishments as warehouses, stores, permanent exhibitions, commercial schools (**Ecoles de Commerce**) and other professionally oriented training bodies providing commercial and industrial courses. In addition, the CCI could administer both sea and river ports and, as from 1933, acquire land or buildings with a view to building airports. State interference and intervention might be increasingly criticized by the employers' organizations but they have steadily been quite ready to assume for themselves responsibility for the running of important elements of public infrastructure and services which have often gone beyond purely local interests and acquire national and even international dimensions, e.g. the international airports in towns such as Nice, Marseille etc.

The ports were the first items of infrastructure to arouse the interest of the CCI, mainly because the very first CCI were formed in towns depending on maritime trade for their prosperity. With the advent of steamships and more costly facilities, the CCI were asked to contribute to the financing of the ports. Because of their considerable and growing financial involvement, the CCI eventually obtained authorization to take over the running of all port operations. By extension, many other forms of public facilities have been created and managed by the CCI, including passenger, commercial and fishing ports, marinas, river ports, nearly a hundred airports; bus stations, industrial zones, motorway service stations, car parks, sportsgrounds, the Mont Blanc Tunnel and the Toncarville bridge. Some CCI collect the '1 per cent logement', another payroll tax used both to fund the building of HLM (*habitation à loyer modéré* – a council dwelling) and to provide loans to employees for house purchases.

In the field of training the CCI are a major provider, ranging from apprenticeship schools to the Ecoles de Commerce, which still retain their early title but are now closer to business/management schools in their philosophy and teaching. All were founded on the basis of the provision of a market of appropriately trained employees for the companies operating within a CCI's area. As many of the member companies are small and therefore ill equipped to provide their own training, this was seen as a fitting role for the CCI. Like many of the airports which now serve an international network, some of the schools created by the CCI have acquired an importance and prestige which transcends national borders, e.g. HEC (**Hautes Etudes Commerciales**), ESSEC (**Ecole des Sciences et Statistiques Economiques et Commerciales**), and ESCP (**Ecole Supérieure de Commerce de Paris**), the top three Paris business schools which come under the control of different CCIs in the Ile-de-France Region

and the **Groupe ESC Lyon** (Ecole Supérieure de Commerce) administered by the Lyon Chamber of Commerce.

Many of the **ESCAE** (Ecole Supérieure de Commerce et d'Administration
des Entreprises) network of regional business schools dating back to the
mid-nineteenth century have also acquired national prestige. At this pre-
experience training stage (**formation initiale**) the CCI run courses leading
to the craft qualification of **CAP** and **BEP** in Ecoles Techniques, apprenticeships in **centres de formation d'apprentis** (apprentice training centres),
technical *baccalauréat*, and higher technician (**BTS** – *brevet de technicien
supérieur*) courses and finally the prestigious engineering qualification
diplôme d'ingénieur in engineering schools (**écoles d'ingénieur**). The CCI
were relatively late (nineteenth century) in establishing engineering
schools, however, at a time when France was already well endowed,
which explains why they control relatively few.

In continuing education (**formation continue**), too, the CCI are major
providers and far outstrip comparable programmes run by Ministry of
Education establishments. Open, public courses, in-company programmes
and training consultancy are all offered by organizations which have
long been considered more in tune with the requirements of business.
The Paris CCI alone possesses twenty-eight different establishments
covering the whole range of training needs.

Services
These include computerized documentation centres and libraries providing surveys and technical assistance. In the regional CCI there are scientific and technical information centres which are primarily intended to
assist the PME with information on licences, patents, products, processes
etc. Technical assistance to struggling PME has considerably increased,
ranging from helping to arrange bank loans to inter-company cooperation.

The Chambers of Commerce financial resources

The CCI's principal source of income is a tax on local companies called
les centimes additionnels, which guarantees a certain level of independence in keeping with their original vocation and essentially because the
state is thus not obliged to fund them out of the national budget. The
intention was to make companies pay directly for the services and facilities they enjoyed through the CCI. The term *'additionnels'* is used to note
that the tax is based on and in addition to the local business rate (**la taxe
professionnelle**). Here lies the real power of the CCI and true source
of their independence, the fact that they can rely on a regular source of
funding which allows them to offer and develop their considerable range
of activities. The reverse side of the coin is that it is also a licence to print
money as the public authorities are powerless to control increases in the

tax so raised, except by changing the Act of 1898. Indeed, during the period 1960–79 the tax rose at an average 20 per cent per year, with considerable variations from one CCI to another.

The **taxe d'apprentissage** represents another major source of revenue which is devoted entirely to the *formation initiale* and *formation continue* activities of the CCI. Many of the *écoles de commerce* rely heavily on this tax, too, and often appoint special staff whose task it is to encourage local businesses to pay the tax directly to the schools. In fact, companies have a number of choices: to pay it directly to an approved training establishment, pay it to the CCI, or use it for internal training. If these three options do not exhaust the sum due, the surplus is forfeited to the Treasury, although in reality most of the CCI ensure that the tax is spent locally and hence have become important tax collectors.

Similarly, the compulsory training tax levied on all companies employing more than eleven can be paid to the CCI up to a limit of 10 per cent of the total due. As with the *taxe d'apprentissage*, companies have a number of choices on how to spend the tax and again the CCI ensure that little is forfeited to the Treasury. Lastly, the CCI charges fees for its wide range of management and other courses and this, too, provides an important slice of revenue. All in all, then, the CCI enjoy considerable wealth, which makes them, as employers' organizations, powerful actors in local and regional economies in terms of services, training, infrastructure and facilities. Central government has on a number of occasions fretted over this financial independence but has always baulked at undermining what is undeniably a major component in regional development.

Conclusion

The year 1995 could well be a major turning-point in the history of the CNPF, with the election of its new president Jean Gandois. The real danger seemed to be coming from Claude Bébéar, the head of the powerful insurance company Axa, who headed a faction of younger employers within the CNPF, whose main aim was to jolt the organization out of its consensus-seeking torpor which had led the CNPF to compromise too much with the unions over the *régimes sociaux*, the social security schemes covering pensions, sickness and unemployment. They claimed there was no real democracy in the decision to prop up AGIRC, the *cadres'* complementary pension scheme, by agreeing to an extra 80–90 bn Ffr over the next ten years in social charges to make up its shortfall. The mainstay of the CNPF, the UIMM (**Union des Industries Minières et Manufacturières**) backed Gandois, the ex-head of Péchiney, however, in the belief that he would be less likely to seek the consensus so scorned in

Périgot's style. Gandois had the backing of both Chirac and Balladur because he favoured further extension of contractual agreements, strong unions and renovation of the **paritarisme**, the joint management by unions and employers of the social security system. For both the national and the CNPF president the biggest task is the same – how to tackle the excessives of social provision whilst at the same time maintaining social harmony amongst an increasingly fractious workforce and trade union movement. There is some paradox in the notion that it is also time to foster stronger trade unions.

For the Chambers of Commerce, no internal strife exists of the kind splitting the CNPF. Their consultative and representative role has considerably waned, maybe in deference to the CNPF, in favour of an extension of their practical involvement in local and regional communities. Their financial muscle ensures their place as an important source of assistance and know-how to their business catchment areas.

8 Business and the making of business people

France boasts an excellent tradition in nursery school education. Only Belgium has higher participation rates among the 2–6-year-old age groups. The **Ecoles Maternelles** are intended for children aged 2–5 years. However, every 3-year-old in France has a statutory right to nursery education and over two-thirds of parents of 3-year-olds avail themselves of this opportunity. By the time French children have reached the age of 5, the overwhelming majority attend an Ecole Maternelle. Eighty-five per cent of all Ecoles Maternelles are in the state sector. Private nurseries also thrive in a country whose appreciation of the importance of the academic 'profile' of an individual has no equivalent in the European Union.

Primary education

Compulsory education begins at 6 and ends at 16 in France (see Appendix 1). The local communes are responsible for establishing and maintaining **Ecoles Primaires** where children spend five years sub-divided into two sets of a two-year and three-year period. These sets are known as **cycles** and involve the children in 27 hours per week of classwork covering nine half days, including until recently Saturday mornings in most regions. The total number of hours varies from week to week but the subjects studied at this level are constant and include French, mathematics, a foreign language (a maximum of 3 hours foreign language teaching was introduced experimentally in some schools in September 1989 for pupils in the last two years of primary school), science and technology, history and geography, 'civics', art, art/music education, physical education. Approximately 18 per cent of the school population between the ages of 6 and 12 are taught in private schools, and this issue of private education was fiercely contested during the late 1980s, particularly at secondary level as it challenges the basic tenets of education in

France being secular since the creation of the Third Republic. The issues of contention were, however, more to do with the stratification of French society and the resourcing of public sector institutions rather than a resurgence of anti-clericalism (most of the schools in the private sector are **confessionnelles**, i.e. maintained by religious bodies – principally the Catholic church).

Secondary education

After five years in the Ecole Primaire, French school children move into the **Collège d'Enseignement Secondaire (CES)** where they will spend four years. This period is sub-divided into what are called the 'Sixième' and 'Cinquième', known as the 'observation cycle', and the Quatrième and 'Troisième' being the 'orientation cycle'. A similar number of hours of attendance are required in the Collèges as in the Ecoles Primaires.

After the Cinquième pupils can elect to follow different forms of education: a pre-vocational class (**CPPN**), a pre-apprenticeship class (**CPA**) or indeed a preparatory year for the vocational **Lycée Professionnel**.

On successful completion of the Troisième at the Collège, pupils are awarded the national certificate called the **Brevet**. Normally, pupils finish the Collège at the age of 15 and proceed to a Lycée or a Lycée Professionnel where they must remain in full-time education for at least one further year. Approximately 25 per cent of all pupils attending a Collège are based in the private sector.

Pupils who have completed four years at the Collège and who wish a more vocational education may move into the first year of a **BEP (Brevet d'Etudes Professionnelles)** or into certain **CAP (Certificat d'Aptitudes Professionnelles)** courses in the Lycée Professionnel. The number of contact hours rises significantly between work undertaken in the Collège and that in the Lycée, where between 31 and 36 hours of classes are the norm. The two qualifications, the BEP and CAP, are essentially different in orientation. The CAP is awarded for specific competence in one trade or craft area. The BEP focuses on vocational skills not for a specific trade but for a specific sector (industrial/commercial/administrative). In the late 1980s it became possible to progress from these basic level qualifications to a technological *baccalauréat* which includes a minimum of 16 weeks' work experience and focuses on one of more than twenty specialist areas.

Another form of Lycée exists which focuses on general education rather than vocational education. This type of Lycée takes pupils from the Collèges and in a period of three years prepares them for the *baccalauréat*. They enter what is known as the Second, First and Terminal classes. The courses followed in the First and Terminal classes are substantially different depending on which type of *baccalauréat* is chosen. There are currently some seven types of baccalauréat, and these are designated as belonging to a 'general series' or a 'technical series' (see Appendices 2–5).

General Series
L   literature (arts-based)
ES   economics and social sciences
S   science
Technical Series
STT   science and tertiary technologies
STI   science and industrial technologies
STL   science and laboratory technologies
SMS   medical and social sciences

These series have now replaced the old groupings of subjects which are still frequently referred to, however, and will figure on CVs of older employees:

General baccalauréat:
Bac A Arts   (now L)
Bac B Economics   (now ES)
Bac C Maths/Sciences   (now S)
Bac D Maths/Natural sciences   (now S)
Bac E Science and Technical   (now STI)
Technical baccalauréat:
Bac F Industrial techniques/medico-social/music/dance   (now STI, STL, SMS)
Bac G Administration, business studies, commerce   (now STT)
Bac H Computers   (now STI)

All *baccalauréat* examinations have written, oral and practical tests. Although the general *baccalauréats* do not prepare people directly for a career, they do enable them to continue their studies, either at universities or in special preparatory classes for the Grandes Ecoles. There are no marks awarded for continuous assessment.

In 1985 France introduced the **baccalauréat professionnel** which requires students to spend a quarter of their time in industry to obtain a qualification which would enable them to enter the world of work directly but also entitle them to go into higher education. The first cohort to 'graduate' with this vocational *baccalauréat* did so in 1987 and numbered 800. In 1993 some 52,500 students passed this *baccalauréat*, demonstrating how popular the qualification is becoming in France as students attempt to escape the stigma of the CAP which enjoys little social prestige and is associated with what the French call 'selection by failure'. Parents and students alike viewed the Lycée Professionnel as some kind of dustbin, as the source of ultimate humiliation in status terms, with 'you'll go to the LP' being viewed as a dire threat to those not making the grade in the more general education options.

The 1989 Education Act set the target of 80 per cent of each year group (63 per cent in 1994) reaching *baccalauréat* level by the year 2000 although, in 1994, this figure was set somewhat lower at 72 per cent in 2003. This ambitious target contrasts with figures in previous decades: in 1950, 5 per cent of the year group passed the *baccalauréat*, in 1960 11 per cent of the year group, in 1970, 20 per cent of the year group. This dramatic increase in numbers of French students passing the *baccalauréat* reflects the concerted but somewhat doctrinaire effort by French governments over recent years to develop a highly-qualified workforce to make France more competitive on the world scene. Greater emphasis is also being put on increasing the numbers of those repeating a year at the Collège, at present on average 10 per cent of a given class. The balance is shifting, therefore, from an unquestioning reliance on the *baccalauréat* to an insistence on gaining a more solid grounding in the basic subjects at the Collège level, and a growing reliance on more students leaving the system earlier to take up apprenticeships.

Higher education

Students who have passed the *baccalauréat* and wish to proceed to higher education can register at university without normally having to satisfy any other entrance criteria other than that of having passed the *baccalauréat* satisfactorily. If they are considered to be of above-average intelligence, they may choose to start a process of preparation for entrance to the French Grandes Ecoles, often nicknamed the **voie royale** (royal way) to the top in both business and society. Grandes Ecoles are institutions outside the university system specializing in professional training for which candidates must pass entrance exams. To prepare for these entrance exams, students normally follow an access or foundation course called the **Classes Préparatoires** which may often be undertaken in the Lycées and requires students to follow two years of courses before taking the competitive entrance examination, the **concours**. There were 73,000 students registered for these examinations in France during 1993.

The Classes Préparatoires aux Grandes Ecoles (**CPEG**) are of three different types.

Science CPEGs are normally followed by people who hold a science *baccalauréat* and follow what is principally a mathematics programme called, during the first year, **maths sup** (*mathématiques supérieures*) and during the second year **maths spé** (*mathématiques spéciales*). This stream can lead to entrance examinations for the engineering Grandes Ecoles or the commercial Grandes Ecoles. Secondly, those who hold arts and science *baccalauréats* and who want to follow careers in non-scientific/non-commercial areas would follow an arts CPEG programme, lasting two years. Lastly, those students holding either a science or economics *baccalauréat* who want to pursue a career in commerce/industry follow a commercial CPEG which lasts for a minimum of one year and are then entered for the examinations of such schools as the **Ecole des Hautes Études Commerciales** (HEC), the **Ecole Supérieure des Sciences Économiques et Commerciales** (ESSEC), the **Ecoles Supérieures de Commerce** (Sup de Co) and the **Ecoles supérieures de commerce et d'administration des entreprises** (ESCAE). To qualify even to be admitted to a CPEG programme students have to submit a dossier from their Lycée and are selected on the basis of academic record and school report. This action constitutes the first selection process for the Grandes Ecoles.

Reform of the CPEG is currently under discussion, the principal changes being extending the commercial CPEG to a compulsory second year and bringing more variety, particularly 'engineering science', into the second year (*maths spé*) of the science CPEG, thereby reducing the amount of time devoted to mathematics, the one overriding obsession of the French education system and a subject which has dominated the selection procedure into both the engineering and the business schools.

Before turning to an in-depth survey of the Grandes Ecoles as a pivotal part of the development of managers in France, it is worth noting that there is no tradition in France of recruiting arts graduates into management and that emphasis is primarily put on mathematical, technical and quantitative skills, implying that management is all to do with analysis and systematic thought rather than collaborative, social interaction and consensus factors.

Technical universities

Technical universities were created in 1969 in response to a demand for shorter technical education programmes than were currently on offer within the traditional university system. These technical universities are known as **Instituts Universitaires de Technologie** (IUTs). They normally award a technician diploma (the DUT – **Diplôme universitaire de technologie**), which is obtained after two years post-*baccalauréat* study. There are approximately seventy IUTs in France. Two-year post-*baccalauréat* courses (Bac +2) are also available in Lycées leading to a qualification similar to, but more narrow than the DUT. This is the **Brevet de Technicien Supérieur** (BTS), in which there are over 100 specialisms. In the main, holders of the DUT and BTS are recruited at the supervisory (**agent de maîtrise**) and technician grades. Many have virtually cornered production management posts which engineers shun for design offices and R&D. They are highly praised by employers and there has been relatively low unemployment at this grade. Precisely because of their increasing importance, however, they have aspirations to *cadre* status, but having reached the top of the technician grade, many find it impossible to become *cadres*, which is reserved for the more generalist engineers – 'you can't have a plethora of generalists in a company, you've got to have some rank and file'. Some large companies have grasped the nettle, however, and particularly prompted by the findings of the Decamps Commission report, instigated training programmes allowing technicians to gain an engineer's qualification or implementing a policy of bringing their status closer to that of engineer and *cadre*, even if they do not have the same responsibilities. Rigid differentiation is still the order of the day in some of the older, large companies, however, and is yet one more symbol of the attachment the French feel for rights and privileges accorded to status and positions, differentiated by educational qualifications. Even the French language allows for such distinctions, the form *tu* being used instead of *vous* in some design offices by engineers when talking to non-*cadre* technicians, to denote their inferiority (*tu* was always used to address servants and is still used to insult).

Universities

Some seventy traditional universities also exist in France which have a non-selective approach to admission of new students – the only criterion being possession of a baccalauréat. This 'open door' policy leads to large numbers of students abandoning their studies in the first year of their programme, either because of inability to maintain performance or a lack of commitment to the course of study initially selected. With 1.3 million students in higher education in France, the university sector represents the lion's share of these registered students, with approximately a million students enrolled in the state university system. We have already noted the two-year programme in technological universities leading to a DUT; an equivalent diploma, a DEUG (**Diplôme d'études universitaires générales**) or the DEUST (**Diplôme d'études universitaires scientifiques et techniques**) is available to students in arts or technical/scientific subjects who wish to obtain a qualification two years after obtaining their *baccalauréat*. That first cycle in higher education is essentially a grounding/foundation programme of study which leads to the second cycle and the possibility of obtaining a **licence** after one year of study or a **maîtrise** after two years of study. Over recent years the *maîtrise* has been rivalled by the establishment of **magistère** or **mastère** qualifications (available also in the Grandes Ecoles) which are often focused on commercial/business/ technical subjects and require a minimum of four years post-*baccalauréat* study. All attempts at introducing selection in universities have failed amidst bouts of student unrest which, after the events of 1968 and 1986, are always calculated to make any French government think twice before introducing radical change into the education system, particularly at university level. Covert selection is in reality practised, however, especially at Paris–Dauphine which rivals some of the more illustrious Ecoles de Commerce in prestige. Because there is no selection, this has the added effect of students studying at their local university, moving through the successive years of their studies with the same friends they knew at the Lycée. Many, therefore, spend weekends at home, and universities consequently do not have the same ethos as in Britain where students see university as much as a 'socializing' and maturing process as a period of acquisition of academic knowledge. This close coterie of friends formed by French students explains much of what is often described by visiting exchange students from abroad as 'unfriendly' behaviour.

The third cycle focuses on research both in terms of methodology and actual implementation of original research leading to different doctorates, the most prestigious of which is known as a **Doctorat d'Etat**, which would normally require a minimum of seven years post-*baccalauréat* study.

The Grandes Ecoles

The history of the Grandes Ecoles in France is both varied and relevant to the profile of modern-day French managers. The first Grandes Ecoles were created in the latter half of the eighteenth century to train civil servants but using science and mathematics as the basis of the education delivered at these institutions. The French Revolution promoted the importance of scientific competence as the major tool in shaping social progress. In the technical domain, a new wave of Grandes Ecoles occurred during the second half of the nineteenth century with the industrial revolution in France revealing the need for competent technical specialists. The 1950s saw the most recent creation of engineering schools, particularly in the area of electronics and technology. The important thing to remember is that these Grandes Ecoles – the most prestigious being Polytechnique, Centrale, Mines and Ponts et Chaussées – although primarily engineering and scientific in their focus, develop people whose capacity for assimilation, intellectual rigour, synthesis and abstract problem-solving give their graduates the ability to adapt to commercial, financial, administrative activity in a number of widely differing sectors. A number of commentators have suggested that the engineering Grandes

Ecoles in France have, in fact, traditionally filled a void in terms of developing managers by being essentially 'alternative business schools', a fact which may explain the relative lack of prestige of the MBA qualification in France, although an engineer with an MBA from one of the American Ivy League or major European business schools can command a considerably higher salary.

The first business school to be established in France was the **Ecole Supérieure de Commerce de Paris (ESCP)** which was established by the Paris Chamber of Commerce and Industry in 1819. The next major landmark in the setting up of commercial business schools was the founding of the Ecole des Hautes Etudes Commerciales (HEC) in 1881. The Paris Chamber of Commerce's example was followed by other regions during the closing years of the nineteenth century, to the extent that by 1900 there were ten regional commercial business schools. By the late 1920s American influence on the French management education system was beginning to be felt, and with the founding of the **Centre de Perfectionnement aux Affaires** (CPA) in 1930 a new emphasis was detectable in the area of developing experienced managers as much as a focus on developing graduates to be managers. France was then in a foremost position in Europe in terms of management education, with the UK establishing Henley and Ashridge Management Colleges only after the Second World War, and, indeed, on a private rather than state basis. The use of case studies and the American influence on management rather than organizational/quantitative factors, led to the creation of the **Centre de Recherche et d'Etudes des Chefs d'Entreprise** (CRC) in 1954 and the **Institut Français de Gestion** (IFG) in 1956.

The founding of **INSEAD** in 1958 was the high point in importing American management education techniques to France, although it is not a part of the French education system. However, INSEAD wanted to be much more than an imitation of Harvard or Princeton Business Schools, seeking more fundamentally to develop groups of international managers expert in international business.

The boom period of the 1960s created a flood of new private business schools in France whose viability and status were more to do with their ability to project and market themselves than the quality of their faculty members or industrial sponsors.

Following 1968, the university sector acknowledged the need to improve its expertise in management education, and in traditional French style, the French government encouraged the French Employers Federation (the CNPF) to fund the training of management teachers by sending over 600 managers to American business schools during the period 1970–6. The government also recognized the need to require companies to develop their workforces rather than to hope that they would do so of their own accord. Accordingly, in 1971 a law was passed stipulating that each company had to draw up a training plan and submit it to its *comité d'entre-prise* (works council) and that each company with more than ten employees would be required to spend at least 1.1 per cent (now 1.3 per cent) of its payroll on the training and developing of its people.

One of the essential characteristics of a Grande Ecole education today is that the student does not need to specialize in terms of selecting from a limited curriculum, until he/she has completed the first two years of a three-year programme. The breadth of the first two years means that in effect emphasis is still placed on the assimilation of knowledge under pressure and the learning of analytical method rather than necessarily the honing of a subject specialism. In addition, the evolution of courses of study in the Grandes Ecoles has been notably towards the inclusion of some social sciences and foreign language skills as well as a strengthening of placements in industry (**stages**) which act as opportunities for testing and applying the knowledge gained in the classroom situation.

With the recession, a considerable number of questions have been asked over both the viability and utility of the Grandes Ecoles system. There is nothing new in this. Literature on business, management and education topics over the past twenty years is littered with attacks on the French *'exception'* of educating what is unashamedly called the *'élite'*, on the tyranny of mathematics and on the sorts of skills and competences the system teaches. The present bout of criticism is different for a number of reasons. First, graduates of the Grandes Ecoles are experiencing unheard-of difficulties in finding the jobs which the system led them to believe were there for the asking. Many have had to accept fixed-term contracts (**contrat à durée déterminée** – CDD) in a tight market where they no longer enjoy a monopoly and employers are becoming more discriminatory and less convinced by the quality of education received. Second, the annual number of *ingénieurs diplômés* produced will have increased from 16,230 in 1991 to 19,950 in 1995, a rise of 22.9 per cent, precisely at a time of downturn in demand. Many directors of the 219 Ecoles d'Ingénieurs (1992) believe in market forces and healthy competition but the added cost of this rise in supply both worries the education authorities and raises doubts over the long-term viability of some establishments. Third, other sectors of the system are beginning to make their mark, as more and more students opt for a management course at university, rather than pay the sharply increasing price demanded at the Ecoles de Commerce (30,000 Ffr for each of the three years of study) as they have expanded and invested rapidly on the prospect of higher demand. Lastly, the system of the **classes préparatoires** is not only undergoing reform but is seriously challenged by schools now recruiting directly candidates with university or IUT qualifications. Although still regarded by many as being a valuable asset and producing the right sort of high-calibre engineers and managers of the future, the realities of the labour market are such that there is no longer an unquestioning acceptance of the Grandes Ecoles system, interrupted only by intermittent but hitherto spurious attacks, mainly from those people who are products themselves of the system and therefore have had no real interest in introducing change. Employers particularly are forcing the pace of change and are gradually but surely breaking the mould of the privileged few who took the *voie royale* of the Grandes Ecoles.

It is only within the past twenty years that post-experience programmes have been widely taken up by French managers. Previously the very fact of attendance at a Grande Ecole would have been sufficient in the eyes of the individual and his/her manager to obviate the need for any further formal education. However, skills in management and professional updating have risen high on corporate agendas in France. The training budget which previously was spent principally on initial and technical training has been increasingly devoted to the 'perfecting' of necessary workplace skills and knowledge. Indeed, the very title of the CPA (Centre de Perfectionnement aux Affaires) reveals this belief in the final 'polish' rather than the necessity for a fundamental education in management.

Vocational training

As we have already seen, vocational training begins in the Lycées Professionnels and continues post-16 in the acquisition of a Brevet de Technicien.

Government legislation in 1992 and 1993 in the area of apprenticeship was an attempt at re-evaluating the importance of apprentice learning in the workplace. With only some 230,000 apprentices following initial training (compared with approximately 1.3 million students following courses in technical and vocational Lycées) the French government decided to enhance the status of apprentices by raising the pay available to them and making much more flexible the length of apprenticeship contracts and the subject matter of which they have to demonstrate their understanding and ability to apply in a practical way. Apprentice training may be carried out in the company itself or an approved training centre. All apprentices have to be registered at a training centre (**Centre de Formation à l'Apprentissage**) and 0.6 per cent of the total 1.5 per cent now required from employers in terms of contribution to training and development in their company is dedicated to apprenticeship training. However, in reality, much of the money allocated to apprenticeship (the **taxe d'apprentissage**) finds its way into company support for training and school institutions as well as to some Grandes Ecoles rather than necessarily to funding/developing apprenticeship schemes.

Normally apprentices in France have to be between 16 and 25 years, and their contract will usually last between one and three years (most contracts last for two years). These apprenticeships lead to state qualifications in the relevant area. A number of French employers have complained recently that apprentice legislation has swung too far in the direction of helping the apprentice and does not take into account the realities of a company's need for short-term return on its employees' activities. Apprentices spend a significant amount of time in theoretical training which is considered to be part of their working week and they have the same legal rights as those secured by permanent employees. They are paid on a sliding scale related to the national minimum wage and employers are able to claim back salary paid for time spent in theoretical training and are not required to pay social charges for apprentices while they are under contract, although a single grant paid on recruitment is under discussion. A noteworthy fact in discussion of apprenticeships in France is that just under a third of all apprentices are women, which is an improvement on the situation in the mid-1970s when just under a quarter of apprentices were female.

Although there was triumphant celebration by the government over the dramatic increase in the number of new apprenticeship contracts signed in 1994 – one of the cornerstones of Balladur's education policy – it is too soon to know whether this is the beginning of a new belief in the value of apprenticeship or a sign that the recession is over in France. In artisan activities, certainly there is little change and some sectors, such as car mechanics, have reported huge drops in popularity. The main uplift, encouragingly, has been in manufacturing industry across all sectors but, nevertheless, industrial apprenticeships only account for 10 per cent of the total. Perhaps the most significant development has been the increased number of higher qualifications beyond the CAP/BEP being obtained via apprenticeships – the *bac professionnel*, BTS and even *diplôme d'ingénieur*. Also new is the ability of the Lycées Professionnels to offer apprenticeship sections, normally hitherto the preserve of the CFA. The government's target, modelled on the example of Germany, is 300,000 apprentices in the year 2003, an increase of 40,000 from 1993–4.

A major preoccupation of the French government over the past few years has been to minimize the possibility of substantial numbers of unemployed remaining unskilled and therefore in a vicious circle of short-term jobs – long-term unemployment. Training courses which cater for those people with no vocational qualifications or who have not had significant work experience are funded by the government and allow for theoretical training combined with practical through-the-job training. When it was first conceived, this scheme focused on those aged 25 and under. However, given the recession, this form of training has been extended to older people who have been unemployed for some significant time. Employers are given a number of financial incentives to encourage them to employ these people and currently just under 3,000 people are following one of these schemes.

The first scheme is geared to enabling people aged 16–25 to acquire a qualification through a mixture of training and practical work experience which is carried out either at a state institution or in a private training organization. The company ensures that the trainee receives a salary which is a percentage of the national minimum wage and that there is a real possibility for the individual to be offered full-time employment at the end of his/her contract which normally lasts between 6 months and 2 years. Since youth unemployment in France is the highest in Europe – 25 per cent of those aged between 16 and 25 years, some 700,000 in all out of a total youth working population of 3 million – the major emphasis is still on finding employment for the young. The **APEJ** scheme introduced in 1994 (**aide au premier emploi des jeunes**) aims at giving the young their first job and offers 2,000 francs a month to firms offering such jobs for a minimum of 18 months, but paid at least at SMIC level. It is only one in a long line of similar schemes targeting the young, stretching back over the last twenty years, from the Contrats Emploi-Formation in 1975, the Plan Avenir Jeunes in 1981, the Travaux d'Utilité Collective in 1984 and culminating in 1993 in the ill-fated **CIP** (Contrat d'Insertion Professionnelle), which allowed for initially paying the young less than the SMIC and which hence sparked off another decisive confrontation between the government and the young, who took to the streets in protest.

A vast mix of measures is available, ranging from exemption from paying all or part of social security charges, tax credits, reimbursement of 50–60 francs per hour of training, the state part-paying the salary of a tutor/trainer and the possibility of deducting training costs from the obligatory *taxe d'apprentissage*. Such a plethora of aid does have its negative effects, however, principally that of being so numerous and complex that companies have considerable difficulty in understanding which measures to use in which circumstances – **contrat d'apprentissage**, **contrat de qualification** and **contrat d'adaptation** being just a few schemes which closely resemble each other. But the government is claiming a gradual improvement in youth unemployment, due certainly in part to its schemes but also to the upturn in the economy and demographic factors such as the gradual fall in numbers in age ranges since the late 1970s. A number of large groups – Accor, L'Oréal, Crédit du Nord, SNECMA, Schneider – have played their part, too, by signing agreements with the government to create more jobs for the young, particularly by providing 'sandwich' schemes (**emplois en alternance**), whereby working time is divided between the job and a course in a training centre. Such agreements are doubtless not entirely altruistic but they do underline that companies as well as the government are seriously concerned about the level and effects of high youth unemployment.

Those people who have been out of work for some time and need to enhance their skills and knowledge before returning to the marketplace can be offered fixed-term or indeed permanent contracts by employers who receive a lump sum for each of this kind of employee as well as the reimbursement of any training costs and the usual exemption from social charges. There are minimum periods allowed for hiring such people.

An aptly named scheme called **Contrat Emploi-Solidarité** offers unemployed people the possibility of 20 hours per week work and training with 85 per cent of the costs covered by the state. This time, however, employees receive a full national minimum wage.

Other schemes exist which are intended to ensure that no unemployed person lacks the opportunity to gain new skills through training. The cost to the French government is enormous, but there is a belief that the return in the longer term will also be substantial.

The French Civil Service has led the way in recent years, in terms of establishing a minimum of 2 per cent of the total payroll costs to be spent on training. As noted earlier, the national minimum currently stands at 1.3 per cent with, however, many companies in the private sector greatly exceeding this figure. It is calculated that some 3.2 per cent of payroll costs was spent by private sector companies in France in the period 1992–3. In the civil service sector, employees are entitled to a minimum of 3 days' training per year and any reorganization of departments or rationalizing of the workforce gives rise automatically to training actions agreed with the employee on a 'full-salary' basis.

Many of the training schemes described above have been integrated into agreements on a sectoral level. These agreements can lead to innovative arrangements such as an incremental entitlement of employees to training after a certain number of years service. This entitlement is portable from company to company within a specific industry sector.

Sectoral level agreements are re-enforced at company level. Every five years, a substantial review has to be undertaken by each industry area in terms of the nature, extent, focus and output measurements, relating to the training of its employees. At company level, companies are bound to hold several meetings each year to discuss the specific training needs of employees, current measures being taken to address these needs, the balance between personal and professional development and the responsibility of the company for ensuring that skills are achieved through actions in working time.

Legislation demands that each employer must draw up a training plan on an annual basis if they have more than ten employees. Consultation of works councils is also required by law but it should be noted that this is more of an information sharing action, in the majority of instances, than a true dialogue. Most companies wish to determine the criteria for training and the evaluation of that training as the responsibility of management rather than a collective responsibility. The tension of increased worker participation in defining training needs is likely to grow substantially over the next few years in France.

It has been estimated that a quarter of the working population in France (i.e. some 5 million) receive some form of training on an annual basis.

One of the most interesting aspects of training in France is the entitlement of an individual to a **Congé Individuel Formation**, which gives the right to up to one year of full-time training or 1,200 hours part-time training outside the company. The individual must have been employed by the company for a minimum of twelve months and have had at least two years' professional experience before being eligible to apply for such leave. Due notice has to be given to the company to allow it to accede to the request or deny the possibility to the individual (but the company must provide reasons for its refusal, in this case). As can be readily understood, this form of leave is not broadly welcomed by employers who do not determine the nature of the training to be followed and can only accept or reject a request from an individual and are not supposed to influence the individual's choice of training orientation.

French methods of financing and structuring training in industry have been cited as examples of government intervention encouraging employers to abdicate their responsibility to define, structure and meet their own training needs without the artificial stimulus of a levy raised on their payrolls. It was commonplace to hear in French industry during the mid-1970s (shortly after the introduction of the training levy) that training and development was increasingly a means of 'keeping individuals and the *comité d'entreprise* happy'. It was also noted that smaller companies used to pay the levy direct to a training organization without actually undertaking any training themselves, finding it too difficult to release people from a small workforce to undertake formal training. Since those days, however, the return on investment in terms of monies expended on training and development has become much better defined, and the integration of training as a means of achieving the strategic intent of a company has become recognized by both line managers and human resources professionals in France. Smaller companies are now availing themselves of not simply external training inputs but also increasingly seeking to develop their workforce through the job and also avail themselves of the numerous schemes which exist to strengthen their workforce by bringing in unskilled but well-funded individuals capable of being developed to meet the precise needs of the company. These schemes also enable companies to hold what might be called 'an extended interview' with people whom they may wish to retain on a longer contract. There is still, however, much that needs to be done in the small to medium-sized enterprise area to strengthen the skills of employees.

A profile of managers

France, like many other European countries, is geographically, socially and culturally diverse. Traditionally, however, France has chosen to englobe this diversity through a centralized, systematic and codified structure, with Paris not merely as the hub, but, in reality, the pivotal point around which both regional and national planning revolve. Efforts have been made in recent years to decentralize some of this authority to other regions but the impact has been more cosmetic than real. French business life, particularly in the manufacturing sector, has taken its cue in organizational structure from national political institutions and processes. The vertical authority, defined and exclusive areas of responsibility, visibly confident and powerful hierarchies and centralized planning in companies, mirror the wider social and political structures. The paradox, however, is that French managers are extremely good at circumventing rules and regulations while apparently paying lip service to them. This contrast between the apparent need for collective, legalistic parameters and the strong need for individual action are features of French business life which merit further examination.

It has become commonplace over many years to compare the stratification of French management to the military environment from which the term *cadre* was originally derived. The most interesting aspect of this comparison is that the relative positions of people in the 'management pyramid' are determined by their educational qualifications more than by their skills profile. There is, then, a need to return to the definition of *cadre* to explore the resonance of the term in modern-day business. *Cadres* have been described as 'a buffer group between workers and employers' and, indeed, a definition as general as 'those enjoying some level of authority'. Previously, it was a simple affair to define what *cadre* meant: normally someone graduating from a Grande Ecole would be able to enjoy *cadre* status from the outset of his/her professional career, simply due to the fact that such a graduate would have spent a period of five years in continuous study after the *baccalauréat*. However, in today's society, with the service sector exploding in importance and the mushrooming of small to medium-sized businesses in France, this definition based on education alone is grossly insufficient to accommodate the status of self-made entrepreneurs lacking formal educational qualifications but evidently successful in French business life. There are, however, legal factors which need to be taken into account in the definition of *cadres* such as the specific retirement arrangements for *cadres*, their 'probationary' periods and their nationally defined right to monthly remuneration.

The Anglo-Saxon term 'manager' suggests control, some might say 'the ability to cope', with teams at work and the necessary resources to achieve stated targets. A *cadre*, on the other hand, is normally perceived as an individual responsible for interpreting corporate vision and strategy, channelling the work of others and structuring that work, to achieve corporate objectives. There is a greater moral 'charge' to the word *cadre* than to the term 'manager'. A *cadre* is part of an organization's framework and is normally also, at an early/middle stage of his/her career, a **responsable**. A *responsable* has a defined area of authority and accountability. Reliance is placed on the personal and professional integrity of the individual *responsable* to achieve specified objectives and each one tends to take or leave whatever he/she wants according to their own personal perception. *Responsables* work with others but are essentially individually accountable and this focus on the individual is at the heart of the particular form and processes of team working in France.

The educational development of a French engineer stresses the individual's capacity for sustained and pressurized work and the ability to analyse effectively and to formulate clearly the crucial points relating to any argument. Before entering the Classes Préparatoires the individual will have been 'selected'. Before being admitted to the Grande Ecole the individual will have been 'selected' through an extremely competitive examination process. These two selection barriers give the individual not merely a reassuring sense of ability but also an awareness of being part of an élite. Self-reliance rather than delegating to others, refining a personal focus on a problem or issue rather than seeking the perspectives of others on the same point, expediting actions or expecting others to expedite actions without necessarily involving others to give them a sense of 'ownership' in the process – these are some of the traits of an education system which demands substantial individual effort and rewards that individual focus accordingly. Increasingly, however, Grandes Ecoles are requiring students to take part in team project actions, consultancy teams working on particular issues identified by a client company, and, more generally, the social aspects of managing people.

Over two-thirds of French managers interviewed in a survey in the late 1980s believe that a business organization is essentially a 'system of authority'. Geert Hofstede has demonstrated that this widely noted phenomenon in French organizations of explicit and strong hierarchical delineation is more to do with organizational points of reference than it is to do with control of an individual's work. French managers need to know what is required of them and to whom they are accountable. They do not, however, view intervention by their boss as a normal, necessary and integral part of his/her responsibilities. On the contrary, they would view such intervention as not merely interference but also a questioning of their professional integrity, which we have already noted is an important part of the moral profile of French managers.

The process of recruitment to managerial posts in France can be divided between large companies recruiting dozens if not hundreds of graduates each year and the smaller enterprises taking only a few entrants. Larger French companies tend to operate their recruitment procedures by direct contact with Grandes Ecoles through a **Forum** which may itself be organized by the Ecole or several Ecoles working in consortium at which companies are given the opportunity to present themselves and their career development policies. Such events would normally take place among the 'top divisions' of the Grandes Ecoles whereas students at Grandes Ecoles considered less 'worthy' by some would send in their application letter to a number of these companies directly. Students attending the most prestigious Ecoles can expect to have several offers of employment during their final year and are normally able to pick and choose among the offers. There is still a trend towards employment with large French-headquartered international companies with a certain amount of networking undertaken by previous graduates from an Ecole to ensure continuity of entrants from their former institution. This has undoubted advantages in terms of a common set of values and language but its disadvantages are even more numerous: that of a lack of international experience and perspective, a strengthening of the sense of loyalty to a single firm and, therefore, a possible complacency of believing one has a job for life; a lack of openness to entrepreneurial/operational skills as opposed to academic qualification; and insufficient internal promotion opportunities for less academically qualified, but nevertheless very competent, colleagues who are currently at technician/supervisory level.

From their earliest days in the company, young French managers discover the need for formality in their relationships with others, not that social distance is encouraged for its own sake, rather that it appears that close personal relationships could be manipulated to distort clear demarcation lines of responsibility/accountability. This desire not to 'confuse the personal with the professional' is yet another indication of the need in French business for reducing to a minimum ambiguities that can be avoided. The fear appears to be that the individual will suffer in such a relaxed and informal situation as these rights and identity are subtly undermined by a form of friendly corporate consensus. There are, of course, companies in different sectors in France where informality is greater than in other sectors. Even in those companies, however, the use of the personal *tu* does not reduce the social distance entirely and in cases of dispute, people will revert to individual role specification rather than collective seeking to achieve a corporate goal.

Relations between industry and government are strengthened by the tradition of the top graduates from different Grandes Ecoles being offered posts as assistants in ministerial offices. They pursue their careers in the French civil service, confident in the knowledge that at a time identified by them they will be able to move into a senior level appointment in French industry. This mobility, sometimes described as **pantouflage**, i.e.

the 'parachuting' of an experienced civil servant into a very senior post in industry and government, is enhanced by the fact that **anciens** ('old boys') from the same Ecoles are frequently in informal contact and maintain an effective communication flow to the benefit of the state and the companies concerned. Secondly, there is an appreciation on both sides of the dimensions of issues and their implications for both parties. Thirdly, it facilitates the enactment of state initiatives in infrastructure development. It also means, however, that some of the more senior appointments made in French industry are of extremely capable and well-connected individuals whose knowledge of the operational realities in the company or sector concerned may be, unfortunately, extremely limited. The fact that this process is not as commonplace as it used to be but that its evident worth has been proven on several occasions, suggests that the innate ability of these gifted individuals more than compensates for their lack of company-specific experience.

Conclusion

More books are read in France on training and development and, in particular, on management development than in any other country in Western Europe. It is significant that this search for knowledge is expressed in a country whose substantial efforts in skilling its people have brought it to the realization that training and development is an example of a perpetual motion phenomenon, 'the more you know, the more you know what you need to know!' There are significant social consequences to the stratification of French education and, indeed, the way such education, training and development impacts on the style and attitudes of managers in French companies.

Throughout the 1980s, the major thrust of government policy was quantitative in the belief that the upskilling of the nation could be achieved purely by increasing the numbers taking the *baccalauréat*. Present policy is more qualitative in the realization that different forms of education, training and qualification are required both for individuals and for corporate requirements. More emphasis on upgraded vocational courses and particularly on apprenticeships has hence been the result.

At higher education level, the well-entrenched system of the Grandes Ecoles is yet again under fire as it is realized that, in spite of its undoubted successes, the type of person it produces and the nature of the courses it provides may now no longer meet with the requirements of the world of work. Companies are increasingly calling the tune in a tight labour market but it remains to be seen whether the system can cope simultaneously with the mini-explosion in the number of engineers being produced and the competition from rival courses at universities.

Appendices

Appendix 1   French school structure and examinations

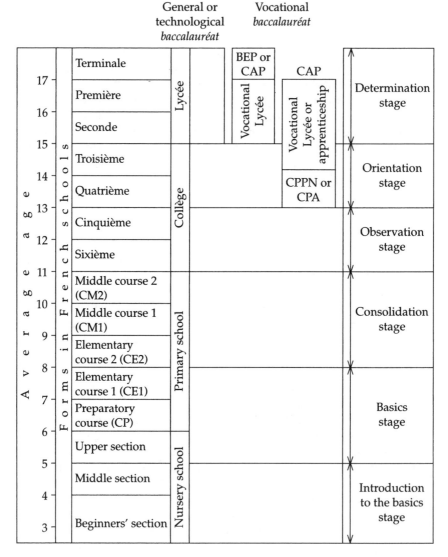

BEP, Brevet d'Etudes Professionnelles; CAP, Certificat d'Aptitude Professionnelle; CPPN, pre-vocational class; CPA, pre-apprenticeship class.

Appendix 2 Baccalauréat series

The tables below show the components of the seven *baccalauréat* series published to date.

Series L (literature)

Main subjects
French (first class)
Philosophy (terminal class)
First modern language
History–geography

Subsidiary subjects
Mathematics (first class)
General science
Second modern language or classical language or artistic subjects (i.e. musical education, fine arts and architecture, theatre etc.)
Physical education/sport

Series ES (economics and social sciences)

Main subjects
French (first class)
Mathematics
Economics and social sciences
History–geography

Subsidiary subjects
First modern language
Philosophy (terminal class)
Second modern language
Physical education/sport

Series S (science)

Main subjects
Mathematics
Physics and chemistry
Life and earth sciences or industrial technology or biology–ecology (agricultural training)

Subsidiary subjects
French (first class)
Philosophy (terminal class)
History–geography
First modern language
Physical education/sport

Series STI (science and industrial technologies)

Main subjects
Construction engineering
Industrial technology systems
Physics and applied physics

Subsidiary subjects
Mathematics
French (first class)
Philosophy (terminal class)
History–geography (first class)
First modern language
Physical education/sport

Series STI (science and tertiary technologies)

Main subjects
Economics–law
Public relations and organization/management (in first class)
Management and programming and application of computers (diversification according to chosen fields in terminal class)

Subsidiary subjects
French (first class)
Philosophy (terminal)
Mathematics
First modern language
History–geography
Physical education/sport

Series SMS (medical and social sciences)

Main subjects
Health and social sciences
Communication in health and social services
Human biology
Physiopathology and medical terminology (terminal class)
Subsidiary subjects
French (first class)
Philosophy (terminal class)
Physics
Mathematics
First modern language
History–geography (first class)
Economics (terminal class)
Physical education/sport
+ compulsory option (terminal class)
Preparation for competitive examinations for health, social or office automation sectors

Series STL (science and laboratory technologies)

Main subjects		
Laboratory physics and industrial processes	Laboratory chemistry and industrial processes	Biochemistry and bioengineering
Physics	Physics	Biochemistry
Electricity	Practical physics	Microbiology
Measuring and automation	Chemistry	Human biology (terminal class)
Computer applications (terminal class)	Practical chemistry	Physics
Applied chemistry	Technology and chemical engineering	
Optics and physical chemistry or monitoring and control of processes		
Subsidiary subjects		
French (first class)		
Philosophy (terminal class)		
Mathematics		
History–geography (first class)		
First modern language		
Physical education/sport		

9 Business and enterprise

Introduction

There is no legal definition of small and medium enterprise (**PME** – *petites et moyennes entreprises*) in France, but PME (or often **PMI** – *petites et moyennes industries*) is usually employed to denote companies not exceeding 500 employees. They also include companies with less than 20 employees and thus represent 99.9 per cent of the total number of companies (see Figure 9.1 and Table 9.1). Fifty per cent are owned and managed by one single person, 48 per cent employ between 1 and 19 and only 0.5 per cent employ between 100 and 499. They create 50 per cent of total value added and employ two-thirds of salaried workers – 8.6 million out of 13 million in 1991.

During the 1980s, as in many other countries, they were considered to be the new spearhead of both industry and services, creating 450,000 new jobs whilst large companies lost 870,000. In this same period, they accounted for 46 per cent of investment, 30 per cent of research and 25 per cent of exports (excluding the defence industry). Starting in December 1991, the trend has been dramatically reversed, with the PMEs losing more jobs than they are creating, with even the healthiest companies affected. In the three years 1990–3, 150,000 went into liquidation after twenty good years, especially for those employing less than 100. It was expected that 1993 alone would see over 70,000 companies disappear. With banks hesitant to lend, the situation has been made even more acute, even for the specialist credit providers such as the CEPME (**Crédit d'Equipement des PME**), which provides long-term loans for PME and whose capital has recently been increased by 5 bn Ffr by the government.

Start-ups in France

One of the big reasons for the high company mortality rate in France is quite simply that more companies are being created – 207,000 between

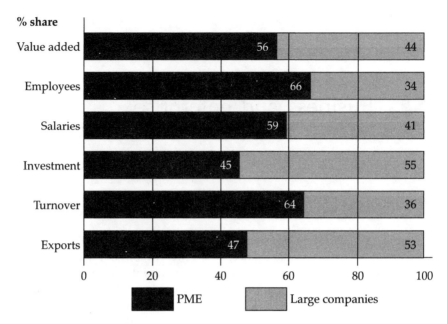

% share

Figure 9.1 *Relative importance of PME and large companies. Source: Le Monde 6.7.93, p. 28*

1986 and 1991, compared with 164,000 between 1981 and 1985. It is therefore perhaps not surprising to see the failure level rise after years of strong growth, the mortality rate being 56 per cent of new companies four years after start-up in industry, 53 per cent in services and 40 per cent in commerce. A contributing factor has also undoubtedly been that in a climate which, after years of denigration, established the world of business as acceptable and respectable, many amateurs with no business experience were lured into setting up a company by the euphoria of the boom period of the late 1980s.

Favorite sectors were commerce, building, hotels and restaurants. In the latter case, for instance, with more and more people eating out, France has witnessed a rapid increase in the number of fast-food chains, e.g. McDonalds, Quick, and the specialist patisserie chains such as Lenôtre. The surprise has been the number of senior managers in their early forties applying to set up their own McDonalds franchise as a way of using their experience to build an independent future. In 1992 alone, some 3,500 applications were received, with the total number of McDonalds standing at 240 in 1992. Sub-contracting, too, enjoyed a huge increase in the 1980s, accounting for 37 per cent of PME in 1980, rising to 60 per cent in 1990, as large companies increasingly 'externalized' certain activities (computing, market surveys, training etc.).

Table 9.1 Numbers of companies by size of workforce in France (in thousands)

	0	1–19	20–99	100–499	Total PME	Large companies
Industry	74.9	110.5	22.5	5.0	212.9	1.0
Building and civil engineering	147.6	157.3	9.3	1.0	315.2	0.1
Commerce	268.1	296.4	14.7	1.6	580.8	0.3
Transport and telecommunications	45.1	27.9	3.9	0.6	77.5	0.1
Services	52.7	438.3	17.7	2.7	980.4	0.4
Total no. of companies	1,057.4	1,030.4	68.1	10.9	2,166.8	1.9

Source: INSEE

Sub-contractors of the large groups have been precisely the first to be hit by the economic downturn, however, being especially vulnerable in that many over-rely on just one or two large customers. The drop in investment in 1992 in particular had a big effect, with orders taking longer (over six months on average) to decide and hence stretching payments to suppliers. Before the recent recession, on average PME paid at 90 days with large companies paying at 70 days. Under the Act of 1992, although difficult to enforce, there are now penalties for late payers amounting to one and a half times the official base interest rate. For many companies, however, the problem is not just one of final direct payment but also one of discounting by the banks. Many business payments within France are made by bill of exchange (**une lettre de change, un effet de commerce,** or, more commonly, **une traite**) which can be discounted by the banks if suppliers wish to receive their money before redemption date. With the increase in company failures and their own diminishing profits, banks have become more and more reluctant to provide this service, even when the customer is a government department, as happened recently when a bank refused to discount a bill drawn on the Direction Générale de l'Armement. On a general note, a code of good conduct on sub-contracting is being actively discussed by the government.

Finance

For many new companies, development has been replaced by survival, particularly for the more innovative enterprises where the options are stark – more working capital or bankruptcy. One new mechanism has been provided by the specialist agency OSFARIS, the French risk capital insurance fund for PME which has created a new fund of 300 million Ffr to insure banks giving medium and long-term help to healthy PME. Although banks are often charged with being timorous and expensive (a typical overdraft of 100,000 Ffr for a PME would attract 14 per cent interest) in general, most demands are usually met, with bank aid to PME over the past fifteen years growing faster than GDP. The basic problem is that those that are healthy are not investing and those that are unhealthy are those in difficulty with the banks.

The government, too, has not been slow in providing help through quicker repayment of VAT, cheaper FDES (**Fonds de Développement Economique et Social,** the state-run organization originally financing companies meeting national planning objectives, principally through low-interest loans), loans for companies in difficulty, an increase in CODEVI (**Compte de Développement Industriel** – bank savings scheme whose proceeds are earmarked for industry) ceilings, the new SOFARIS fund and lower social charges for lower salaries, principally by transferring the cost of family allowances from companies to the state budget.

Many observers have remarked, however, that the whole financing structure (subsidized loans, CODEVI, specialist institutions) needs restructuring to become more transparent and user-friendly and that it lacks the coherence and efficiency found in the USA, Germany and Japan. Indeed, some go further and blame this incoherent structure for the numerical weakness of middle-size companies (employing 100–500) of which there are only 5,000 in France compared with 6,000 in the UK and 8,200 in Germany. It is a widely felt belief in France that more of this size of company (part of the so-called *Mittelstand* in Germany) are urgently needed since these larger PME provide more security and dynamism and are the best shock-absorber for recession.

In the early stages of development, a variety of sources of finance exist, ranging from the founders of companies, their families, hire purchase, leasing and external suppliers of equity finance (Figure 9.2) show that one big difference between the UK and France is the far lesser extent to which overdrafts are used in the latter case and the concomitant greater reliance both on short- and medium-term loans. Overdraft and short-term finance is used only to meet immediate working capital requirements. Overall, 22–32 per cent of finance comes from the banks and 51–60 per cent from earnings in France, as opposed to 21–23 per cent from banks and 65–77 per cent from earnings in the UK.

Venture capital (**capital-risque**) has now swapped its name for investment capital (**capital-investissement**). As in other European countries this reveals a drop in support for expensive and risky young companies and a greater concentration on more mature companies, particularly those with a succession problem as the original founder approaches retirement age. Providers of venture capital in France have been particularly anxious through this shift of focus to emphasize their image as long-term partners and thus put paid to their reputation of speculators buying cheap and reselling at a much higher price.

Venture capital expanded rapidly in the UK after being imported from the USA but took longer to take off on the continent. It is still very much in its infancy in Germany but has rapidly developed in the Netherlands, and particularly in France which, with 6 bn Ffr invested annually, is now the world's third largest provider, but way behind the USA which is thirty times larger and the UK where venture capital is twice as big as in France.

The shift from young to more mature companies has been the main characteristic of the past ten years, particularly those seeking a successor. Thus, sums invested in start-ups, currently running at 290 m Ffr have barely increased during this period, whereas overall investment has quadrupled. The fashion for Californian-style high-tech start-ups seems,

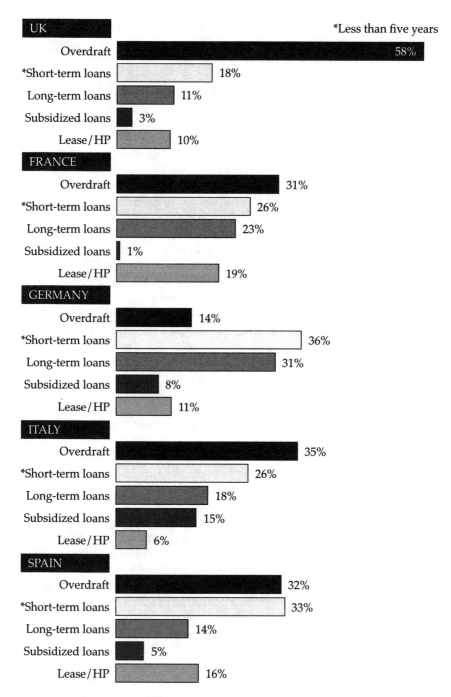

Figure 9.2 *How small firms are funded in Europe. Source: 31 Cranfield Enterprise Centre/Midland Bank*

therefore, to have waned considerably, as money going to buy-outs and succession cases has increased rapidly from 60 m Ffr in 1986 to 2 bn Ffr in 1994.

Finding a successor is becoming crucial to the survival of PME. Some 4,000–5,000 companies a year fail because of a bungled succession, with a further 2,000 disappearing through not finding a buyer. A central problem is the penalizing inheritance tax which discourages family succession. Tax measures favour takeover by outside intersts and therefore jeopardize the survival of those family-owned PME which are so highly praised by the employers confederation, the CNPF (*Confédération Nationale du Patronat Français*). The Hoover case (see Chapter 2) is viewed as showing the limits of being dependent on multinationals.

Around 55,000 companies change hands every year. It has been calculated that 25 per cent of around 40,000 companies with a workforce of 50–1,000 will be affected in the next ten years, as post-war entrepreneurs reach retirement age. If the company is taken over by the founder's family, tax of up to 40 per cent may be payable on the company's value. The more prosperous the company, the more heavily the family is taxed. If it is sold to outside interests however, capital gains tax (**impôt sur les plus-values**) is due at the rate of 18.1 per cent. An additional problem is posed by the French laws of inheritance under which the owners of companies must share any handover equally amongst their children. If two children inherit a company, for example and one has no desire to stay in the company, then he/she must be paid half of the value by the other, the payment of course being subject to the 40 per cent inheritance tax. Hence, the cost of transmission within a family is reckoned to be twice that in the UK because of the tax treatment. There are ways of circumventing the tax issue but many owners fail to lay the ground early enough, hence the comparatively high number of companies which cease to exist. Because of the tax implications (the maximum inheritance tax was doubled from 20 per cent to 40 per cent in 1984), owners now increasingly sell out to large groups. Ten years ago, over 80 per cent of companies stayed in the family but this figure has now dropped to only 50 per cent.

As far as staff buy-outs are concerned (RES – **rachat par les salariés**) again tax has become a major issue, with the tax credit which was once allowed being abolished in 1992. Many well-publicized RES have ended in difficulties. The employees of Darty, the electrical household equipment retailer, contracted debts of 5 bn Ffr over ten years and because they ran into difficulty over paying the debt, the company was taken over by the British company Kingfisher (although to salvage national pride, it was called a merger in France). Goupil, the personal computer manufacturer, and Jeanneau, the yacht makers, both ended up in liquidations, with the employees of Pier Import, the cane furniture and oriental products retailer, selling out to a rival company.

Expansion funds account for 2.5 bn Ffr of investment made by venture capital companies. A common complaint, however, is that, in spite of the comparative success of the **Second Marché** (Second Market), created in 1983 and the equivalent of the Unlisted Securities Market (USM)) in the UK, there is not a powerful enough stock market which would allow both the PME to find other sources of finance and the venture capital companies to be sure of being able to exit when they wish. More has been said of the Second Marché in Chapter 4 on finance, but in the context of the PME it is interesting to note the support given by the French venture capital association (AFIC – **Association Française des Investisseurs en Capital**) to the idea of setting up the equivalent of the American NASDAQ, the over-the-counter market which lists nearly 5,000 stocks. France is no different from other European countries in having strict and tough listing requirements, in particular proof of several years of profitable trading whereas on NASDAQ many high-tech companies have raised large amounts of capital even before breaking even. In 1993 alone, 520 companies were introduced to NASDAQ, 140 to the London Stock Exchange and thirty in the rest of Europe, including ten in France. In the first six months of 1994, however, fifteen companies were brought to the Second Marché, thus underlining the increasing enthusiasm for the Stock Exchange as a source of finance in France.

The main suppliers of venture funds in France are either independent, the main sources being pension funds (3 per cent), banks, insurance companies and other financial organizations (58 per cent), with large companies providing 7 per cent and rich individuals 8 per cent. Public sector providers include the state banks and insurance companies, and a plethora of local and regional bodies, in particular the Sociétés de Développement Régional (SDR) and Regional Councils. In general, the PME in France appear to enjoy a broader range of support from national and local government than their counterparts in the UK. In spite of its shortcomings, the Second Marché plays its part at regional level in this respect too, since the presence of the seven regional stock exchanges appears to favour better and more immediate information for local investors, with local banks and stockbrokers having extensive knowledge of local companies. Additional support in the form of advice, particularly on aid packages, comes from the powerful Chambers of Commerce, generously financed by local taxes, and local branches of the CNPF (see Chapter 7).

For high-risk technology projects, the main publicly sponsored source of finance is ANVAR (**Agence Nationale de la Valorisation de Recherche**), which supports technology transfer, in the main from public research programmes. Its loans are interest-free and only payable if the project succeeds. Again, it is active on a decentralized basis, with large centres having considerable decision-taking powers, in contrast to the

British 'Smart' programme where decisions are taken centrally by civil servants.

As a complement to ANVAR loans, companies may also apply for a research tax credit (**crédit-impôt**). It is relatively easy to obtain, the requirement being for companies to complete a special form when filing tax returns. Under the scheme, companies may deduct 50 per cent of their expected increase in R&D expenditure, taken on a year-to-year basis. A company which invested 1 million Ffr in R&D in 1992 and 1.5 million Ffr in 1993, for example, can set 50 per cent of the added 0.5 million Ffr against corporation tax. Some 6,500 companies benefited in 1992 but a considerable number ran into problems over the necessity to justify claims. Strict records of receipts etc. must be kept, otherwise the tax saved is liable to repayment, with the tax authorities having the right to check on the last three years. A new government measure also encourages PME to hire researchers and *techniciens supérieurs* through a mix of grants and subsidized training periods of up to 6 months. Overall, research funding was spared in the government budget of September 1993, with ANVAR's funds being increased and the *crédit-impôt* being left intact, as France subscribes to the OECD view that there is a significant correlation between employment in high-tech companies and the overall pattern of employment. More employment in high-tech leads to an increase in employment generally. Hence, various high-tech sectors will be identified for priority aid. Biotechnology has already been earmarked with other priority areas to be publicized in 1994.

The CODEVI savings accounts have already been mentioned. These are used in particular to finance the PME at a rate which has recently been lowered from 8.75 per cent to 8.25 per cent. At the same time, the ceiling for savers in these accounts has been raised from 15,000 to 25,000 francs.

Bankruptcies

According to a *Le Monde* report, France is currently the European champion of company failures, with some 70,000 companies failing in 1993 (53,000 in 1991, 9,000 in 1973). The 1985 Act was designed to help companies who decided on a **dépôt de bilan** (voluntary liquidation) to recover, whereas some 95 per cent end up in a **règlement judiciaire** (compulsory liquidation). The basic emphasis of the 1985 Badinter Act was to give companies in difficulty more room for manoeuvre and was particularly designed to save jobs. A new law is now being sought under which the pendulum will swing back in favour of a reinforcement of the powers of creditors.

Generally, there is the suspicion, especially by the banks, that many *dépôts de bilan* are fraudulent and being used to raise funds illegally. The criticism of the 1985 Act are twofold. First, it institutes a period of observation following the *dépôt de bilan* during which the company ceases payments and is protected from its creditors. During this 6-month period, which is renewable for up to 18 months, the company is not required to repay previously contracted debts, which thus leads to the accusation that the Act is keeping many companies artificially alive since eventually so many are compulsorily wound up. This observation period sees debts increase, thus causing a domino effect as other companies, acting as suppliers, are brought down. It is also during this period that asset-strippers move in and take advantage of the law to snap up companies cheaply and sell off at a profit those parts which are profitable and thereby make capital gains for themselves only.

Secondly, any new bank loans or suppliers' credit obtained during this observation period become priority debts over those contracted prior to the *dépôt de bilan*. This in particular provokes the wrath of the banks, since it renders any loan guarantees worthless.

The new law will appoint 'controllers' who would be informed of all offers and takeover bids, but it is generally felt in France that all the legal texts in the world (and there are thousands of them) have not prevented France from being the failure champion of Europe. The law should only help those companies with technical know-how worth protecting and a good customer base but which have cash-flow problems. Any other companies, it is felt, should be liquidated. In addition, more recourse should be made to an amicable settlement as in the USA with the use of Chapter 11. A procedure should exist which will shelter companies from creditors before recovery, but this procedure should be quite open and not highly secretive, as is the culture at present in France. The banks in particular are asking for a review of the observation period following the *dépôt de bilan*, an appeal procedure for creditors and greater transparency in takeover conditions.

The entrepreneurial culture

In some quarters, there is criticism of a lack of creativity amongst French managers. As one commentator has observed, companies are under-led and over-managed. Companies think too much of *diplômes* or qualifications and not enough of the job itself. Partially, the Grandes Ecoles are held to blame for producing precisely a graduate clone, steeped in maths and the exact sciences. In addition, very few engineering schools teach management, and generally there is not enough exploitation of hidden talent. Priority is given to abstract knowledge and logical precision in studies which are highly intellectual and conceptual, a fact which may explain the new-found enthusiasm for apprenticeships and the German 'dual' system.

Between them, Ecole Polytechnique and ENA provide 45 per cent of the heads of the top 200 companies. If HEC is included, the figure exceeds 50 per cent. Taking the next layer of management (**les cadres dirigeants**), 75 per cent come from top category schools (Mines, Centrale, Ponts et Chaussées, ESSEC, with Polytechnique alone accounting for 25 per cent). Selection, as is seen elsewhere, is exclusively based on the sciences and particularly on maths and the system produces hard workers, capable of rigorous reasoning and precision, abilities more likely to lead to meticulous management than imagination and originality. Selection is preceded by the *classes préparatoires* which involve 70–80 hours of cramming per week, in conditions not favourable to spontaneity, curiosity and risk-taking. As a GDF (Gaz de France) Human Resource Director once said, a *polytechnicien* can never be wrong.

Others, however, reply that the system only produces what is required. The classification into the strict hierarchy of company management structures is carried out by the Ecoles themselves. It is not the schools but the rigid hierarchical structure of firms which prevent young managers from being more imaginative and risk-taking. Whether the fault lies with the Grandes Ecoles producing graduates with the wrong qualities or with the companies for asking for the wrong qualities, it is quite clear that there is a general feeling in France that the whole combination of Grandes Ecoles and companies may well militate against the risk-takers and innovators. One promising figure, however, is that 55 per cent of the Ecole Centrale's graduates now work for companies of less than 2,000 and this may well indicate a trend towards seeing the smaller company as being more flexible and creating a more appropriate climate for innovation and creativity.

PME and social charges

There is nothing specific to the PME about the problem of high social charges in France, but their effects are perhaps more keenly felt since it is one of the main causes of the failure of the PME to create more employment and, in many cases, limits future expansion.

France is not specifically handicapped in terms of uncompetitive wages but there is a very marked gap between the salary cost to the company (gross salary + employer's social charges) and the net salary received by the employee (gross salary minus employee's social, i.e. national insurance, contributions). For the same net salary, income tax is much lower than in Germany, in Italy and in the United Kingdom (see Table 9.2), employees' social contributions are high, although lower than in Germany and employers' charges are higher than in both Germany and the UK. In 1991, the share of employers' contributions alone amounted to 31

Table 9.2 *Pay, tax and social security contributions: a European comparison (for an unmarried worker)*

		Italy	France	Germany	UK
1. Gross pay	1979	125	125	146	142
	1989	138	132	155	139
2. Employees' social	1979	11	15	23	9
security contributions	1989	12	23	27	13
3. Income tax	1979	14	10	23	33
	1989	26	9	28	26
4. Net pay after tax*	1979	100	100	100	100
(1–2–3)	1989	100	100	100	100
5. Employers' social	1979	58	47	23	14
security contributions	1989	67	59	27	14
6. Cost of labour (1+5)	1979	183	172	169	156
	1989	205	191	182	153

* Base 100 for net pay.
Source: Micossi and Papi, 1992

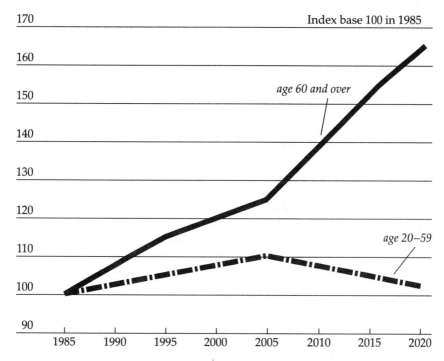

Figure 9.3 *Demography of France. Source: INSEE*

per cent in France, compared with 23.6 per cent in Germany and 14 per cent in the UK. In total, for the same net salary after tax, the cost of labour in France is slightly lower than in Italy but a little higher than in Germany and very much higher than in the UK. Since negotiations are not over net salaries but over gross salaries, the gap between direct salary and the global labour cost has most certainly a psychological effect on employers, which discourages job creation. Recent trends seem to be reinforcing France's specificity with respect to the balance between social charges and taxation and the system of financing the social security system. On the one hand social charges continue to rise (there has even been talk recently of a 'social' VAT to reduce the chronic deficits of the system) and on the other, direct tax contributions are declining.

To reduce the gap, the most natural solution might appear to be to reduce expenditure on the welfare system but the problem is structural in that health expenditure is increasing faster than economic activity and expenditure on pensions is likely to increase rapidly with an ageing population (Figure 9.3). Whereas in the past employees have largely accepted increases in social security expenditure and hence their contributions as a form of state saving scheme to cover their illness and old age, it is not at all certain they will continue to do so. Hence the preferred solution of the Planning Commission in their report *Choisir l'emploi* is to optimize present expenditure through better management and control. This is already beginning to happen, with employees now having to work 40 instead of 37 years to qualify for a state pension, with the final pension being calculated over a greater number of qualifying years. As for health expenditure, doctors are being obliged to prescribe more generic medicines. France lags some way behind most other European countries in this respect with the interests of both the pharmaceutical industry and chemists being well served by the prescription of branded medicines. In addition, doctors are now being strictly limited in both the type and quantity of prescriptions they can give for both medicines (the French being the biggest consumers of medicines in the European Community due to their low cost) and other forms of treatment, e.g. blood and urine tests, cardiographs etc. which are mostly undertaken in private laboratories in France. The net effect is an immediate outcry by both chemists and laboratories, where job losses ironically now seem inevitable, but the general aim is to limit the nefarious effect of social charges on employment as a whole, even if short-term labour market adjustments are necessary.

The Lyon region

One good illustration of the importance of PME to the French economy and the problems they encounter can be found in Lyon where the new TGV station at Satolas airport is predicted in ten to fifteen years to become not only a major meeting point of all TGV lines in Southern Europe but a vast multi-modal hub for goods traffic transported by road, rail and air. In the meantime, however, local industrialists are becoming impatient to put Lyon on the international map, aware that in the USA and Germany much better infrastructure and facilities are available at a local level. There are many small, independent companies in the Lyon region which have now breached the magic barrier of 1 bn Ffr turnover and are becoming aggressively more European, even global, in their ambitions as mini multinationals in the making, in sectors ranging from household refuse treatment, telesurveillance and pharmaceuticals to fresh-food packaging and textiles. In high-tech and traditional industries, such companies are the solid bedrock of the local economy in an area which provides a good market, the largest after Paris and of the right critical size in which to test their products, technology and marketing. Competition is so fierce that if companies survive they may be strong enough to attack first the national then the European market, thus underlining the key reason for the wealth of companies in the area. All the major consultants and providers of venture capital have a base in Lyon, providing services and finance not only to large and medium companies, but particularly to small companies showing promise of development. Siparex is one such source of finance and is typical of the strength of the financial support companies can expect to find at regional level in France. One other company, Louis Thannberger, is one of the best specialists in France in bringing small companies to the Second Marché. The Banque Martin-Maurel, Crédit Lyonnais, the Société de Développement Régional (SDR), Sudinnova, Banexi, Banque Populaire, Lyonnaise de Banque and many others illustrate the plethora of capital providers.

The entrepreneurs of Lyon share little in common with the flamboyance of Bernard Tapie. The typical values cultivated in Lyon are those of hard work, discretion and patience. Application and rigour are the order of the day in a city known for old-fashioned attachment to stolid conservative values but which have served many of its PME well as they have grown into leaders in their sector. Some of the Lyonnais PME are tempted by a quotation on the Bourse, but in keeping with their traditional values, many are not converted to its advantages and prefer slow growth to the explosion that external capital might bring. Typical, too, is the number of local clubs and associations to which the younger generation of entrepreneurs belong and which have slowly assumed more importance than the traditional network of Freemasonry, particularly since the arrival of Michel Noir as mayor of Lyon. He has surrounded himself with the heads of the most dynamic PME to discuss **la nouvelle donne industrielle française** (the new French industrial deal), thus providing an example of the powerful role of economic catalyst played by local mayors, particularly in the larger towns. The accusations of corruption now levelled at Michel Noir are, however, an example of the extent to which this relationship can become incestuous as politics and business become inextricably and unhealthily intertwined.

One fact which typifies the underlying tendency towards centralization in France, in spite of wholesale efforts at decentralization, is the way in which those PME in Lyon which do make the grade, rarely stay in the town to replace the old giants of Renault trucks, Rhône-Poulenc and BSN (France's major food company, now renamed Danone). There is a slow but steady trickle of major decision-centres in the direction of Paris which fuses together the milieux of politics, the administration, finance and industry in a tight web of interlocking relationships from which many companies are loath to be absent, in spite of the strength of local networks.

Conclusion

As in most economies, the PME were seen to be the way forward in terms of growth and job-creation and, throughout the 1980s, they fulfilled their promise. Into the 1990s and recession, however, their progress has faltered, with France now holding the record for the highest number of liquidations, a situation partially due to the laws on bankruptcy which favour owners and employees over creditors.

There is no shortage of finance for new companies, with the government acting promptly to provide help and the regions playing a major role. The whole financing structure has been criticized, however, for lacking the efficiency and transparency of other countries' systems and particularly for failing to encourage the growth of middle-size and family-owned companies.

Two major problems beset the PME at present. As owner-managers retire, a combination of inheritance and income taxes penalize the transmission of a company within a family. Secondly, the prohibitive social security costs act as a certain brake on companies' expansion and particularly on the job-creation expected of them.

Although some would criticize the Grandes Ecoles system for stifling initiative and creativity, in providing graduates more suited for the unwieldy hierarchies of the larger companies, the experience of Lyon proves that there is no lack of aspiring entrepreneurs. Many are testing products on the Rhône-Alpes region before undertaking launches on the national and European markets. They underline the general conclusion that, over time, the PMEs in France have fared better than larger groups, particularly in the traditionally strong areas of luxury goods, food and drink.

10 Penetrating the French business culture

Introduction

Although the French clearly prefer foreign companies to establish themselves within the country rather than simply export to France, for many, particularly small companies, this is an essential first step in testing the market.

Some observations need to be made here which may appear too simplistic and self-evident but nevertheless, in view of mistakes made in the French market, are still worth considering. First, a thorough survey of the French market must be undertaken, together with establishing a means of monitoring changes in regulations, fashions, trends and competitors. Exporters often fail to understand fully the nature of the French market and as far as the product itself is concerned, little regard is often paid to French taste, particularly such features as design and packaging which may often be of a higher quality and require written instructions for use in appropriate French and adapted to French usage requirements.

Second, exporters lack a proper understanding of distribution channels, particularly the more fragmented nature of retail distribution and the complex system of the **grandes surfaces** (hypermarkets, supermarkets) purchasing organizations, their discount structure, delivery and payment conditions etc. The relationship between suppliers and retailers is particularly fraught in France where the latter are increasingly gaining the upper hand. Competition is hence fierce and requires persistence, toughness and, above all, the right price/quality ratio in a market which is highly price-conscious and well supplied by both domestic and imported products. In spite of accusations of protectionism, particularly in public procurement, France is a wide-open market for most products, particularly consumer goods.

Last, the regional nature of French markets is often not fully appreciated. One agent or distributor will often not suffice in a country where pockets of population and industrial activity are far-flung and may need individual and discriminating attention.

Direct selling

With both considerably expanded air and rail networks and the creation of 'nodal' points of trade and commercial activity in Paris, Lille and Lyon, the attraction of direct selling should not be underestimated. Principally, it enables direct contact with customers and hence a constant update of requirements and the ability to control sales. With agents and distributors, there are major contractual difficulties, particularly if it is desired to dispense with their services for failure to develop sales or for over-concentrating on other products which they also represent.

The French market is often very conservative, however, and customers may tend to remain loyal to traditional suppliers. Complete professionalism is therefore required and both a thorough knowledge of French, particular sectors and general French commercial practices (the practice of the mail-shot in English is particularly resented) are vital. The use of English may be widespread but a mastery of French can open many doors and flatter linguistically chauvinist customers.

Certain private companies, such as Euromarché in the retail sector, prefer to deal directly with suppliers based in France or working through an agent. This is to ensure reliable deliveries from local stockholdings and prompt after-sales service from on-the-spot staff. Government departments, such as **UGAP**, the French public procurement agency, will also prefer to buy imported goods through intermediaries such as agents. One solution to such problems is the direct use of warehouses from which the direct seller may supply the market, especially in the case of industries with a high level of spare-parts required.

Agents

For those companies lacking expertise in both French and the French market, the use of an agent (**agent commercial**) will be seen to overcome linguistic, cultural and other barriers. As has been seen, however, severance payments may be high and therefore it is crucial both to have a written contract and to ensure that it covers such items as the duration of the contract (on a trial basis, in the first instance), the specific territory to be covered and the clients to be visited and finally the percentage of commission. A mere handshake and a gentleman's agreement must be avoided at all costs since even oral commitments may be binding. Agents can claim compensation (**indemnité**) if termination is not the result of a serious fault. Good and reliable agents may be found through Chambers of Commerce, overseas accountants and lawyers operating in France, trade associations and through the experience of customers and end-users with agents.

In negotiating with an agent, it is important to bear in mind his or her experience in selling similar lines, their ability to carry stocks, which advertising and promotion costs are to be shared (many expect these to be covered by the principal) and the nature of the agent's sales force, e.g. whether they are single-product VRP (**Voyageur, Représentant, Placier**) or **multi-cartes**, representing more than one product. Many customers prefer the wider range offered by *multi-cartes* VRP.

It is essential, too, to make regular visits to the agent's customers both to prove commitment and to establish identification with the supplier. If technical support is needed, it might be necessary to send someone with fluent French.

Distributors

It has already been noted that one common error committed by exporters to France is to assume that France is one big homogeneous market. In appointing a distributor (**concessionnaire**), therefore (who, unlike the agent, buys and sells on his own account and actually owns the goods before reselling), it is important to challenge any claims he may make to be able to cover the whole country. Depending on the product, it could well be that only certain regions need be selected: Lyon, for consumer goods as a test market, for example. A case in point would be the hyper-market chain Casino which is based in St Etienne and has strong links with many local distributors. Since local authorities, hospitals, schools etc. may practise a covert 'Buy French' policy it may also prove valuable to consider some form of franchise (**une franchise**) agreement whereby the distributor may use his own name on the supplier's products. It is still true to say that often a French name will open many French doors but the obvious downside is loss of brand name associated with a high-quality product. Many distributors will insist on non-exclusivity, too, as far as the range of products they carry is concerned and here care is obviously required to determine whether other competing lines are com-patible with the suppliers' own product. As competition is often fierce in many sectors one major problem in France may not be to find a distrib-utor but to keep him. Hence every effort must be made to serve the dis-tributor well (regular visits, after-sales service, training etc.).

Forming a French company

The simplest form of presence is the branch office (**succursale**), which, in reality however, still requires a considerable number of formalities to be established, such as a translation of the parent company's articles of association to be filed with the Clerk of the Commercial Court (**Greffe du Tribunal de Commerce**) and notification of the branch to the local tax, social security and other authorities. The company's name, commercial lease and translation of the birth certificates of the Président and Branch Manager must also be filed with the Commercial Register (**Registre de Commerce**). A major drawback with a branch, however, is that the head office is liable for all debts incurred and its accounts may be investigated by the French tax authorities in the event of financial irregularities occurring in the branch office.

The major forms of company such as the **SA** and **SARL** etc. have already been covered in Chapter 3, but it is worth repeating here the importance of the term **fonds de commerce**, which is basically the business including goodwill (**clientèle**), the trade name and specific tangible and intangible assets. Since the commercial property (**les murs**) is quite distinct, two transactions have to be made when purchasing commercial property, one for the acquisition of the business and a second for the acquisition of the property. The commercial lease (**bail commercial**) also forms part of the *fonds de commerce* and may be a critical component to ensure continued trading of the company. Again, there are numerous formalities involved which require the services of either a *notaire* or *avocat* to establish the origin and turnover and profits of the *fonds de commerce*.

Acquisition of land

In terms of the acquisition of land, the services of a surveyor (**un géomètre**) will be needed who will register a site plan with the Land Registry (**le cadastre**) which works together with the **Conservation des Hypothèques**. The latter maintains a register of all mortgages and changes affecting a title and contracts for the purchase of land (**un acte**) will be published at the Conservation. If the land is to be developed a VAT form will also need to be completed. The legal function of the *notaire* is to make out contracts, witness signatures, collect and distribute the purchase price and register the transfer. He works for both parties but remains impartial and independent. For land and property purchase there is a preliminary agreement (**un compromis de vente**) at which stage a deposit (**des arrhes**) is due and a sales contract (**acte de vente**). Completion and signing of the contract are simultaneous in France.

Crucial to the purchase of land is the existence of a land development plan (**Plan d'Occcupation des Sols** – POS) in every commune and in which the mayor is heavily involved and wields overriding control. Courting of the mayor is essential, therefore, not only for this reason but also because he is responsible for awarding major contracts and concessions. In this sense, he resembles the PDG of a Société Anonyme in that there are few checks and controls on his power, a situation which has led both many mayors (and members of parliament (*députés*) who are allowed to hold office as mayors at the same time) and businessmen to be charged with abuse of public funds. The whole area of public procurement, and particularly the accusations of awarding concessions to the large water companies on a personal basis, has led to demands for greater clarity and accountability in the relationship between local administration and business.

Mergers and acquisitions

In France, most purchases into other companies take the form of minority and majority stakes. Full acquisitions are still comparatively rare. Majority stakes of 50 per cent are quite common with a minority stake involving the purchase of 10–50 per cent. Concert parties holding more than 33 per cent of a company's equity must launch a full bid, however.

In addition, employees, trade unions and workers councils (*comité d'entreprise*) have statutory rights to be consulted over any change of control but they do not possess any right of veto. French companies can also place important restrictions on the transfer of shares either by contract or in the articles of association. Common ploys are double voting rights issued to shareholders holding shares for more than two to four years, non-voting preferred equity, which can represent up to 25 per cent of share capital, and investment certificates which have limited transferability and can again represent up to 25 per cent of share capital. Even more crucial is the existence of cross-shareholdings which are both permitted and widespread, with the tacit agreement that they will not be used to launch takeover bids. In reality, they are often used to thwart bids.

Hence, unlike the UK where a thriving securities market is encouraged to sanction bad management, in France there are significant and observed limitations on the transfer of both ownership and control. Very few incumbent senior managers lose their positions in the event of their employing company being taken over by another.

Hostile takeovers, too, are somewhat rare although it is predicted by stock exchange specialists that their number will increase as the Paris Bourse grows, both with the flood of privatization flotations and the advent of pension funds. The acquisition of a listed company would typically involve informing shareholders of the intention to purchase either for cash through an **Offre Publique d'Achat** (OPA) or for securities via an **Offre Publique d'Echange** (OPE). The offer must be for at least 10 per cent of the target company or 5 per cent in the event of the share capital exceeding 10 m Ffr. Many target companies will be untested and special care must be taken to collect accurate information. There is a long tradition of both hidden assets and liabilities in France (for tax reasons) and it is generally advised therefore to incorporate a new company or, if purchase must be of the shares, the contract must contain extensive bank-guaranteed and watertight indemnifications.

Joint ventures

Where there is agreement to pool resources to exploit products or technology in specific areas where one single company cannot provide the large sums of money involved, a frequent entry strategy has been to form a joint venture. GEC-Alstholm is one of the best examples in the sphere of electricity generating plant equipment and transport but many more are being developed, particularly in the defence-related industries, e.g. British Aerospace Defence with Matra and Royal Ordnance with GIAT. Often the **société en participation** is used or the **groupement d'intérêt économique** (GIE) which is generally a cost not a profit centre in which the liability of members for GIE debts is joint and several. The GIE is normally used for exports, research and development pooling, and joint sales. Where greater legal and tax shielding is required, both an SA or SARL are used.

From a cross-cultural point of view, joint ventures can pose particular problems in that they often involve constant contact between opposite numbers in two companies of different nationality. Visits, meetings, negotiations, telephone calls, faxes and letters are all part of daily routine for many such ventures and hence, it is vital that both parties develop training programmes which sensitize those involved to the different beliefs and habits as well as commercial and managerial practices of their counterparts. Such programmes have been highly successful in GEC-Alstholm, Royal Ordnance and Carnaud Metal Box, for example, and have led to lower levels of frustration and misunderstanding.

A practical example of what might be included in such training is the purpose and function of meetings. For Anglo-Saxons, time is linear and great stress is placed on doing things one at a time and sequentially. In France, time may be described as being more circular, many things are done at the same time and hence meetings may be constantly interrupted, not started or finished on time, participants may come and go as they please and conduct private conversations. Such behaviour may be anathema to Anglo-Saxons but awareness of such a cultural difference can at least prepare and alert non-French participants to a difference of approach and explain behaviour. Ultimately, if joint teams are put together to work on a more continual basis, the aim should be for the team to define behavioural norms on which they can all agree – in this instance, how they can expect each other to approach and behave in meetings.

Meetings may also differ in terms of their perceived purpose, with Anglo-Saxons wanting decisions and action whilst French managers may view them as either an opportunity to exchange information or as a rubber-stamping operation for decisions taken at a higher level. Hierarchical positions may be quite clear in a French meeting, but more blurred and manipulated in an Anglo-Saxon encounter. More formality and correctness of language may be observed in a meeting in France whereas a greater level of informality and colloquial language may be the norm for Anglo-Saxons. Many joint ventures have foundered because there has been a lack of understanding of such basic issues as these and a refusal to recognize that cultural differences can sometimes be a major cause of breakdown, particularly in communications.

The regional environment

Although the importance of Paris cannot be denied, the national regional development agency (DATAR – **Délégation à l'Aménagement du Territoire et à l'Action Régionale**) has achieved over the past thirty years a more homogeneous spread of growth. The results have been patchy but it can nevertheless be said that there are no real pockets of gross deprivation, although the demise of smoke-stack industries in the North-East around Lille and in the East in Lorraine have left their scars.

Apart from Paris, Lyon and Marseille, France is by and large a country of small and medium-size towns which will focus on specific activities and be relatively remote one from the other. An initial regional toe-hold could therefore be necessary before viewing France as one seamless market. Rates of unemployment and growth, the age structure and density of population and particularly communications are all important factors, too. But it must always be borne in mind that the centre of activity may be in a particular region but major *decisions*, particularly concerning new products etc., may still be made in Paris which accounts for 85 per cent of the headquarters of the top 200 companies, 35 per cent of all managers and 60–65 per cent of all research contracts. In the retail sector, however, not all hypermarket groups have their headquarters and buying agencies situated in Paris, and many operate either a centralized, regional or even store-by-store purchasing policy.

When prospecting the various regions, useful organizations to contact, according to French managers themselves, would include: regional banks, regional councils (**conseils régionaux**), Chambers of Commerce, **comité d'expansion économique** (usually attached to the Chambers of Commerce), DATAR, ANVAR (**Agence Nationale pour la Valorisation** de la Recherche – an organization dispensing R&D finance), **Sociétés de Développement Régional** (regional venture capital organizations), trade and professional bodies and both *département* and municipal councils (**conseil général** and **conseil municipal**).

In addition, in particular towns, the **service économique** at the *mairie* can be critical, since it tends to mastermind local business development. When there are wider implications involving several towns or communes, there may exist **syndicats d'agglomérations nouvelles** (SAN) in the case of new groupings of towns, or **syndicats intercommunaux** in the case of longer established cooperative bodies between communes. **Sociétés d'aménagement du territoire** buy and develop land which is then marketed to companies and they can be the biggest source of information on available areas of activity. Lastly, many towns have **associations d'entreprises et d'élus** which are co-financed by companies and local authorities and which are often responsible for promoting a town or region and for welcoming new businesses.

As has been stated elsewhere, local authorities have much greater power than previously to raise and distribute finance and hence represent significant sources of financial and other aid.

Conclusion

Strategies for entering the French market are no different in many respects from those adopted for other countries but emphasis has been placed on the regional nature of France and the vital role played by local and regional authorities. Infrastructure, particularly transport, is crucial in a country which still has many areas which do not enjoy ease of access. Getting to know the mayor, the *préfet* or the *président* of the *conseil régional* is a must since they enjoy considerable personal power.

In terms of acquisitions, although it is predicted that more hostile takeover bids will occur with the expansion of the stock market under the effect of privatizations, the complex set of cross-shareholding structures and devices used to restrict transfers of shares means that the precise rules of the game have to be thoroughly understood.

Finally, the open nature of the French market has been stressed. To benefit from this openness, however, requires a recognition that from many points of view – regulations, government economic and industrial policy, labour relations, education and training – the subtleties of the French business culture must be clearly analysed and appreciated.

Bibliography

Albert, M. (1991), *Capitalisme contre Capitalisme*, Seuil.

Barilari, A. and Guédon, M.-J. (1989), *Institutions Politiques*, Sirey.

Bishop, M. and Kay, J. (eds) (1993), *European Mergers and Merger Policy*, Oxford University Press.

Bridgford, J. and Stirling, J. (1994), *Employee Relations in Europe*, Blackwell.

Capital, Le, various issues between 1992 and 1995.

Cohen, E. (1992), *Le Colbertisme 'High Tech'*, Hachette.

Commercial Litigation in France, Lovell White Durrant.

Debbasch, C. and Pontier, J.-M. (1989), *La Société Française*, Dalloz.

Deguy, M. (1985), *Seuils d'Effectifs et Obligations de L'Employeur*, Les Editions d'Organisation.

Duhamel, A. (1993), *Les Peurs Françaises*, Flammerion.

Economist, The, various issues between 1992 and 1995.

Entreprise, L', various issues between 1992 and 1995.

Etat de la France, L', 1994–95, Editions La Découverte.

Express, L', various issues between 1992 and 1995.

Ferner, A. and Hyman, R. (1992), *Industrial Relations in the New Europe*, Blackwell.

Gordon, C. *et al.* (1991), *Franc Exchange*, Pitman.

Hampshire, D. (1993), *Living and Working in France*, Survival Books.

Handy, C. *et al.* (1988), *Making Managers*, Pitman.

Iribarne, P.D'. (1989), *La Logique de l'Honneur*, Editions du Seuil.

Lane, C. (1989), *Management and Labour in Europe*, Edward Elgar.

Lessem, R. and Neubauer, F. (1994), *European Management Systems*, McGraw-Hill.

Magliulo, B. (1980), *Les Chambres de Commerce de l'Industrie*, Que Sais-Je?, PUF.

Maitland-Hudson, A. (1991), *France: Practical Commercial Law*, Pearson Professional.

Mémento Social, Le (1988), La Revue Fiduciaire.

Mermet, G. (1992), *La Francoscopie 1993*, Larousse.

Monde, Le, various issues between 1992 and 1995.

Montaldo, J. (1994), *Mitterand et les 40 Voleurs*, Albin Michel.

Mouriaux, R. (1992), *Le Syndicalisme en France*, Que Sais-Je?, PUF.

Nobes, C. and Parker, R. (1991), *Comparative International Accounting*, 3rd edn, Prentice Hall.

Nouvel Economiste, Le, various issues between 1992 and 1995.

Randlesome, C. *et al.* (1993), *Business Cultures in Europe*, 2nd edn, Butterworth-Heinemann.

Brunhes Report (1993), *Choisir L'Emploi*, La Documentation Française.

Raynaud Repart (1993), *Evaluation de la Situation Sociale*, La Documentation Française.

Reichman, C. (1995), *Les Belles Lettres*.

Szarka, J. (1992), *Business in France*, Pitman.

Scheid, J.-C. and Walton, P. (1992), *European Financial Reporting, France,* Routledge.

Somers, F. *et al.* (1991), *European Economies*, Pitman.

Trompenaars, F. (1993), *Riding the Waves of Culture*, Nicholas Brealey.

Tyson, S. *et al.* (1993), *Human Resource Management in Europe*, Kogan Page.

Vincent, J., Guinchard, S. *et al.* (1991), *La Justice et ses Institutions*, Dalloz.

West, A. *et al.* (1992), *The French Legal System*, Fourmat Publishing.

Index